"AND OUR NEXT SPEAKER IS…"

What an accountant, an engineer, and a coach can teach you about public speaking

by

Kam McQuay (the accountant)

Rick Drumm (the engineer)

Dan Kapsalis (the coach)

Bloomington, IN

authorHOUSE®

Milton Keynes, UK

AuthorHouse™
1663 Liberty Drive, Suite 200
Bloomington, IN 47403
www.authorhouse.com
Phone: 1-800-839-8640

AuthorHouse™ UK Ltd.
500 Avebury Boulevard
Central Milton Keynes, MK9 2BE
www.authorhouse.co.uk
Phone: 08001974150

First published by AuthorHouse 7/16/2007

ISBN: 978-1-4259-9641-3 (e)
ISBN: 978-1-4259-9642-0 (sc)

Printed in the United States of America
Bloomington, Indiana

This book is printed on acid-free paper.

CONTENTS

INTRODUCTION

And our next speaker is... YOU!

What is this book all about?

Even the most experienced presenters get anxious before they speak. Will they be effective? Will they be able to convey their message? How will the audience respond? If only there was a way to absolutely ensure that *your* presentation would be successful.

We believe there is. The success of your presentation should not be a chance event, but a collection of processes that gives you the greatest probability of accomplishing your objective.

Throughout this book, we will explore basic — but critical — steps and processes that, when followed, will give you the tools to be successful in your next presentation opportunity. Our goal is to focus on direct and simple methods that almost any speaker can use to conduct clear but effective presentations.

Who are we?

This book is written by three guys who have spent a number of years in the trenches. We are not professors, nor do we make our livings delivering speeches. We work in professions that, like so many others in this world, require us to give presentations on a regular basis. As we witness the quality of presentations at conferences, training sessions, and other professional settings, we feel there is a need for improvement. We want to help.

How will this book help you?

Dynamic speakers are usually credited with some innate ability to connect with their audience and deliver inspiring messages. These intangible abilities are looked on as individual personality traits, usually bestowed at birth, that allow these people to be effective. Nothing could be further from the truth.

Delivering an effective presentation is part message, part organization, part preparation, and part personality, but all of it learned. Conveying an inspiring and effective message is not reserved for only the gifted. It is a learned skill that can be mastered by anyone who is willing to put the time and effort into studying the craft.

Much has been written on how to give effective professional presentations. What this book offers is sound, practical advice from people who have been there. The chapters of this book include plenty of advice on small steps to take, as well as more complicated techniques for effective presentations.

We suggest you read sequentially through the chapters. However, if you look at the table of contents and see a chapter that hits home to you, feel free to start there.

After reading this book, you will be prepared to move on to the next level in your skills. You will be more confident. You will feel more at ease, better prepared, and more able to bring creative, interest-sparking elements into your talks. Since most professionals are required to make presentations as part of their job function, this book will also help your career.

How do we know all this stuff works? Well, we've been there, and still are. Take it from us, an accountant, an engineer, and a coach, if we can learn how to speak effectively, you can too.

CHAPTER 1
THE FOUR E's OF SPEAKING

EEEE! What a way to start!

A man, an expert in his field, had a dream. He was captured by aliens who took him to Planet Zoltar. He was then forced to make a professional presentation on what he did at his job. The aliens provided any and all equipment – computer (with PowerPoint), projector, screen, even some props from his workplace. He had plenty of time. The aliens also made it clear that if he made an admirable presentation, he would be returned to his home unharmed. But if his presentation was not up to standards, sorry; the rules of their planet dictated that he would be killed. (Sometimes, aliens can simply be brutal.) Fortunately, our expert awoke just as he was being introduced. But for many professionals, this scenario is very close to the reality they feel when asked to speak in front of a crowd.

Whenever we attend a seminar, team meeting, or conference, we like to observe the behavior and body language of not only the speaker, but also — and more importantly — the audience. Are they engaged? Attentive? Participating? Or do their eyes wander in hopes of finding something more interesting on which to focus? Ultimately, has the speaker captivated the audience or better yet, has the speaker captivated me?

What would it take to ensure a successful presentation?

A Thought from Kam

You know, I never sit in the front row when I attend a conference. Maybe I attended too many church meetings. Maybe it is the culture in which I was brought up. Maybe I am just lazy and don't want to walk all the way to the front of the room. And maybe I am just like everybody else who is afraid to get too close to the podium. But I think the real reason that I never sit front and center is that if the speaker is not very good, I don't want to embarrass him or myself when I have to take that uncomfortable "stroll" out of the closest exit to escape. I truly don't want to walk out on the speaker, but I also don't want to be trapped and have to suffer through a poor presentation.

When people are asked to speak, some get outright scared, most get nervous, and a few feel energized. Every speaker has the opportunity to impact the lives of others. So, how do you make sure that your next presentation will have an impact?

As simplistic as it may sound, the foundation to high-quality presentations are summarized in the four E's of speaking:

Energy
Excitement
Entertainment
Expertise

Energy

Your individual passion and conviction for what you have to say must be matched by the personal energy that you convey to the audience. If you are not excited about what you have to say, why should the audience be excited to listen to you? Energy is more about you and less about your audience. You cannot control how the audience will react to your presentation, especially if the message is unpopular or difficult to process, but you can control the energy level you bring to the topic and how you express your energy.

Regardless of the topic or setting, you must be passionate about your subject and you must convey this passion. Your convictions will be infectious. Passion is so important that we have dedicated an entire chapter (Chapter 20) to this emotion.

Excitement

Excitement is not the same thing as energy. Where energy is about you — the speaker — excitement is all about the audience and their experience with the presentation. Excitement transcends the type of talk or presentation you are giving. Whether a talk is informational or inspirational, an environment of excitement should be a planned element for the audience to experience. We want to re-emphasize the word "planned." While excitement is often looked at as an intangible element, it can and should be part of your planning process.

Your audience is excited when they have a clear understanding why they are there, and why they are looking forward to what you have to say.

In order to raise the excitement level in a room, speakers typically challenge the audience. They are passionate about what they have to say (the speaker's energy) and they convince the audience that they too need to feel passionate about the topic (audience's excitement). They ask questions of the audience, require the audience to think, and continually engage the audience to be willing and active participants in the presentation. Because of this, they invite and lure the audience to become part of the presentation, whether publicly or in their own minds.

Entertainment

Yes, you must be entertaining. And yes, we know that for many, entertaining does not come naturally to you. Still, as a speaker, you never have the right to be boring.

Let us say that again: **As a speaker, you never have the right to be boring!**

We are convinced that no matter what the topic, no matter who the audience, no matter what the setting, people want to be entertained! Yes, entertainment without effectively communicating your point is a waste of time. Still, we have yet to find a topic or situation where an entertaining presentation does not provide for better communication.

Within your own style, you need to be one part informational and one part entertaining. Once again, we believe this is so important that we have dedicated an entire chapter (Chapter 19) to emphasize this point.

Expertise

Simply put, speak on what you know.

Early in his career, Kam was at an industry seminar where he heard one of the best presentations he had ever experienced up to that time.

A Story from Kam

The topic was a detailed healthcare issue presented, unbeknownst to me, by two professional speakers. The two hours flew by as the presenters spoke to a group of two hundred, and we were captivated by the information we heard. At the end of the presentation, like most presentations, they opened the floor up for questions. Big mistake. Sure enough, this highly educated and experienced audience began asking good, but detailed, questions. The answers the speakers gave were evasive and simplistic, and the audience knew it. A great two-hour presentation was discredited by ten minutes of Q and A.

Unfortunately, one's lack of knowledge is usually evident before the question-and-answer period. Amazingly, many people either fail to perform the required research and due diligence, or just don't know how to prepare.

Another Story from Kam

Since I present a lot, I am frequently asked to speak on topics that are not within my specialty or knowledge base. I'm an accountant, so I should know everything there is to know about accounting, right? Early on in my career, I had trouble saying no to these opportunities (and I am sure it was evident in these presentations).

Several months ago, I gave an update presentation on a topic that was on the fringe of my knowledge base. The research and preparation was about three times my normal prep time, and boy, did I complain about it. But I had little choice. I either had to become an "expert" on the topic or decline the speaking engagement.

We have yet to find a topic or presentation where the four E's of speaking did not apply. We use these whenever we present, no matter who the audience, no matter what the topic. Apply these each and every time you speak, and you will be on the road to a successful presentation.

COACHING POINTS

- ✓ Utilize the four E's of speaking in every presentation.
- ✓ Personal energy is what you bring to the presentation.
- ✓ Be passionate about your subject.
- ✓ You do not have the right to be boring.
- ✓ Plan for your audience to be excited about the presentation.
- ✓ Challenge them to become a part of the presentation.
- ✓ Know your topic.

CHAPTER 2
FINDING YOUR OWN STYLE

"I did it my way."

It is not our goal to make everyone sound like, well, us. Each person should find his or her own style. However, avoiding speaking in public is not a style (unless you're a mime). You will be speaking in public. That is the nature of our world today. Apart from your natural style, the essential elements and tools needed to improve your presentation skills are the same.

Some people are more entertaining. Some are more comfortable lecturing, some teaching, some have a more comforting presence; but whether you feel more at ease behind a podium, with more detailed notes, or in a highly interactive environment, everyone needs to combine their natural talents with proper presentation techniques to find their own comfort zone.

A Story from Kam

I was at a healthcare symposium where I gave a one-hour presentation and decided to stick around for the remainder of the day and take in some other sessions.

When I arrived at one session with only several minutes to spare, the room was packed and I had to sit near the front, right in the middle of a row. No escape for me. While I do not recall the speaker's name, he stood about 5'4" tall, weighed about 130 pounds, and was a college professor at a local college or university. He started the session in his squeaky voice with some philosophical comments about the state of the union, and then proceeded, in rather mundane terms, to outline the material we were going to cover. I could not get out of there fast enough. But I couldn't escape. I was going to be forced to spend one hour of my life listening to this guy. Boy, am I glad I did.

I not only learned more about the topic he presented, I also witnessed someone who knew and understood his own unique style and used it to his advantage.

As he began the session, he looked like he came out of a Norman Rockwell painting, but in the end, he reminded me more of Uncle Fester. His drab presentational style seemed to give way to an endearment of his squeaky voice and unusual mannerisms. He effectively conveyed his point, often repeating himself to make sure everyone understood (or at least knew they had missed the point). He also interjected humor against the backdrop of his dreary personality. My two biggest laughs of the day occurred during his presentation.

This speaker was not charismatic, overpowering, interesting, outgoing, or able to carry an immediate presence — but because he knew himself, knew his own presentation style, and was comfortable in his own skin, "Uncle Fester" was an outstanding speaker.

Finding your own style will not only make your presentation more effective, it will also be a calming influence as you prepare to speak. Here are several suggestions on finding your own style:

- Go with who you are. There is no need to push your personality on the audience or try to act like someone you are not. If you are corny, be corny. If you are serious, be serious. If you are direct and to the point, well, be direct.
- Practice talking to people. The best presenters are those who talk with the audience, not speak at the audience. The only way you can do this is by having a conversation with your audience, not "preaching" at them.

- Be relaxed. Initially, don't worry about being ultra-professional, what to do with your hands, or how many "um's" you may say. Over time and as you practice, you can work on these. Instead, stand with confidence and speak conversationally.
- Watch yourself on videotape. This will be both painful and profitable.

There is always a temptation to mimic the behaviors of someone you know to be a successful speaker or to try to apply detailed principles from, say, a book on presentations. This may be helpful. However, the best presentational style is your own. Find your own style, and you will always be comfortable listening to your own voice.

COACHING POINTS

✓ Find your own style for speaking in public.
✓ It is okay to repeat yourself when making a point.
✓ Use your style with good speaking techniques in your presentations.
✓ Practice talking *with* your audience, not preaching *to* them. Stay relaxed.
✓ Don't worry about mimicking others; be yourself.

CHAPTER 3
PRACTICE AND PREPARATION

Mind your P's, but you can forget about the Q's.

The keys to acquiring any skill are always preparation and practice.

Not too long ago, famed NASCAR driver Jeff Gordon was asked to lead/sing "Take Me Out to the Ball Game" during the seventh-inning stretch at a Chicago Cubs baseball game. Things did not go well. Two things became very evident as Gordon attempted to lead the song: 1) He did not prepare. Not only did he not know the words to the song, he introduced himself by welcoming everybody to Wrigley Stadium, instead of Wrigley Field (an insult to loyal Cub fans everywhere); and 2) he did not practice. To put it bluntly, Jeff Gordon couldn't sing. Why in the world would you accept an invitation to sing at a seventh-inning stretch in front of thousands of people and not practice a few bars prior to that day?

> *A Story from Kam*
>
> Not long ago, I was speaking to an up-and-coming department manager who shared with me that she was not as comfortable as she thought she should be when giving departmental presentations. So I asked how many departmental presentations she does in a year. "About one or two," was the answer.

Now, how good are you going to be when you do something only two times per year?

It is the same with speaking. Therefore, to improve your speaking ability, we would encourage you to speak as often as possible.

When preparing for a specific presentation, we encourage you to do the following:

- Review your material and underlying data several times over the course of several days. This is particularly important for technical talks. The flow of a presentation improves when you know the details, and are confident in the facts.
- Take time to review the entire presentation, focusing on the major points and the message you are trying to communicate.
- Always prepare and have more material available for presentation. As a general rule, we suggest having at least one and a half times what is needed.
- For stories or major areas of the presentation, practice by reciting them out loud. Many people recommend practicing in front of a mirror.

A Thought from Kam

Although people often recommend it, personally, I have never been a big fan of practicing in front of a mirror. It is just not comfortable for me. However, it would not be the first time someone caught me talking to myself in my car as I drive to a presentation, reviewing the major sections of my speech for my briefcase and leather seats to hear. I do believe some of my best material was discovered behind the wheel of my car.

- For practice, videotape yourself! Everybody owns or at least knows someone who owns a video recorder. Seeing yourself "live" will help you to identify your strengths and weaknesses, and enable you to evaluate your overall presentation.
- If it is a really important presentation, do a live dress rehearsal.

Another Thought from Kam

When we say *live*, we mean *live*. For some of my biggest presentations, I purposely schedule a local or smaller group session to "perform" the topic a week or two before an important presentation. It is still amazing to me, after all these years, just how easy a presentation is - the second time.

When we look around our culture, we see many, many examples of the importance of practicing a skill. Musicians spend many hours rehearsing on their own, then often as much time with the band or orchestra. Athletes don't just walk on the field and play. They hit the weights, run the sprints, jog the miles, and work on the basics of their sport. Professionals spend time preparing on their own, then with teammates or companions. What is true for the athlete and musician is also true for the accountant, engineer, scientist, doctor, sports manager, businessperson, lawyer, healthcare worker, and any other professional: practice and prepare.

A Story from Rick

I had the opportunity to listen to my endodontist recently. I say "listen" because, since he was giving me a root canal and had numerous awkward and painful-looking devices in my mouth, I couldn't quite say anything, except maybe "Aaaaaggghhh."

He was talking to his assistant about a talk he was giving to a group of dentists the next week. He described how he was setting aside a number of hours putting together material, photos, and even video for the talk. The next week, unfortunately for me, I was back in his chair again, but it did give me the opportunity to ask him how it went. He said that the evaluations showed his talk was well-received. Additionally, hardly any of the dentists skipped his talk and left early on a warm spring day to play golf at the nearby golf course. I attributed this partly to his presenting style, which, from talking to him a short time, I surmised to likely be engaging. But, their interest also had a lot to do with his willingness to spend the time to practice and prepare.

Overall, the two biggest keys to successfully presenting are:

- At every opportunity, you need to be applying your craft in front of an audience. There is just no way you can replace actual "on-the-job experience" when it comes to speaking. So, no matter who the audience, no matter what the subject: stand up and be heard. Practice your craft.

- Review your material... and then review it again. It should be of no surprise that the topics we feel most passionate about and have the most experience with, are the presentations we feel most comfortable with, and are the presentations that are ultimately the most successful. Even for the most experienced presenter, there is a direct correlation between the amount of time in preparation and the success of the presentation.

We can hear — right through the pages of this book — the comment that some readers are making now.

"But I'm not a professional speaker."

Now for the truth: If you make presentations as a part of your job, like the majority of professionals in this world, you are getting paid to make presentations. Therefore, *ipso facto*, and *habeas corpus* (okay, we're not lawyers), you are a *professional* speaker. So act like one and improve your skills.

The old saying "failing to prepare is to prepare for failure" is absolutely true when it comes to speaking in front of a group. On the rare (but memorable) times when we did not deliver a top performance, it was directly linked to the amount of time — or more to the point, the *lack of time* — we spent in preparation and practice.

COACHING POINTS

✓ There is no substitute for the P's: preparation and practice.
✓ Speak as often as possible.
✓ Apply your craft in front of an audience.
✓ Review your material several times.
✓ Practice telling stories out loud.
✓ Study details beyond what your talk covers.
✓ Rehearse for yourself, on tape, or in front of others.

Chapter 4
Collecting Information

Scavenger hunt, anyone?

If you have to give more than a presentation or two per year, as many professionals do, it would be wise to build a collection of diverse materials to draw from as you prepare. There are many different types of information that can enhance your presentation and will prove helpful for use during your time in front of people. We will discuss a few of these here, including research and practices, news articles, pop culture, and photographs.

Research and practices

This is the one area that most professionals seem to have a grasp of, no matter what the topic. There is work being done in numerous places in the world that will support or defend an idea, further an understanding, or give helpful insight into your topic. If you run out of ideas, Google it.

As a highway safety engineer, Rick spends time reading up on research articles about what has worked in improving safety. But here's the key to easier preparation for a talk: *He does this when there is no talk on the schedule.* It not only helps him with his work, but by filing selected articles away, it helps him be prepared for whenever he does have an opportunity to speak.

When Kam speaks on healthcare-related finances or tax issues, he conducts an online search for interesting court cases that have involved his topic. There are, to put it technically, some really wacky ones out there.

This pulls the audience into the topic, lightens the tone, and gets the listeners to be more in tune with what Kam needs to tell them.

News articles

Always be on the lookout for media coverage of events in your profession. Newspaper, magazine, TV news, and the Internet all have things to say about professional issues — and eventually, your topic. Highway crashes seem to be a staple for news outlets; sports has its own section in the newspaper and slot on the evening news. Heck, even accounting shows up in the news at times. Unlike research articles, these pieces are usually written by people who know virtually nothing about your specific topic. But it's okay, because their audience doesn't know much about it either. This may be humorous or it may be sobering. But either way, news items can be great lead-ins and a valuable resource to your presentation.

Pop culture

When talking about how out-of-touch engineers are, the photo of a famous engineering student made it into one of Rick's presentations: William Hung, of no-talent *American Idol* fame. This was, of course, when Hung was making appearances on TV shows and releasing an album that — in technical terms — was considered "very, very bad."

Pop culture is part of everyone's life. Most people, even if they have not seen a hit movie or top-rated TV show, know something about it. The fact that these are popular means many people in your audience have seen them. Making a clever reference to a show or a person in the limelight is a big help in drawing people into your presentation. However, when you do this, make it relate to your topic somehow. Don't mention or make fun of the most recent Hollywood star on trial for some felonious activity unless that goofball majored in your presentation subject, or has some other direct connection to your theme.

A picture is worth at least hundreds of words

Adding pictures to your presentation is helpful. By pictures, we mean any visual form, including photos, drawing, comics, paintings, streaming video, etc. However, we do draw the line at mimes. Well, come to think of it... aahhhhh, no.

Pictures add an element that is often not contained in our professional number-laden, wordy presentations. Pictures are visual elements that add variety and color and help the audience connect to what you are saying.

But from where do we get pictures, photos, and video? Here's a helpful hint to improve your presentations, particularly for those who have very visual topics. Always carry a camera with you. Interesting sights are everywhere. Incorporating pictures that are related to your topic, particularly when they are insightful or humorous, will almost always draw the attention of your audience.

There have been a number of times that we have been on the road and rued — yes, *rued* — the fact that we didn't listen to our own advice here.

A warning about the internet

This warning is not about viruses or spyware. This warning is about using photos and stories from the Internet that *everyone* has seen. You know the ones - the picture that has been e-mailed to you three times this past month, or the story that has circulated through your office (and through the office of every colleague at the conference). Let us clue you in: Everyone has seen it! You might get a chuckle, but most people are thinking, "Been there. Done that. Seen it."

When you look on the Internet for insightful stories or photographs, search for ones that people haven't necessarily seen. The more you have to search to find that great picture or photo, the more likely it will be new to your audience. It is okay to be creative in your search.

A list of resource ideas

By no means comprehensive, here is a list of resources you can use to get ideas for your presentation.

- Publications
    o Research journals
    o Trade journals and magazines
    o News magazines
    o E-zines for your profession
    o Motivational, business, or management publications

- News
    o TV
    o Internet
    o Newspaper
    o Radio

- Pop Culture
    o TV
    o Movies
    o Music
    o Commercials
    o Catch phrases

- Photos or Video
    o Your personal collection
    o Internet
    o TV
    o Movies

- Others
    o Weird news stories
    o Classic literature
    o Famous quotes

The sources are endless. Use ones that you enjoy, and that you think would capture an audience's attention. Have fun and be creative.

COACHING POINTS

✓ Always be on the lookout for material for your topic.
✓ Keep up with research, present practices, the news, and pop culture.
✓ Add pictures or video to your presentation to help make your point.
✓ Use new and creative information, or use common references in creative ways.

CHAPTER 5
HOW TO START YOUR PRESENTATION

"Ta-Da!"

The most important parts of any presentation are how you begin and how you end. Yeah, sure, it would be nice to say something useful and worthwhile in between, but your beginning sets the stage for the entire presentation, and the ending determines the impression you will leave.

This chapter focuses on how to begin your presentation. Chapter 6 finishes this idea with tips on how to end your presentation on a high note.

A Story from Dan

A few years back, I was at a national coaches' convention in Philadelphia. Like many conventions, there are hundreds of topics and speakers covering all areas designed to help you improve your coaching knowledge. With so many topics available, many occurring at the same time, you have to pick and choose the ones you feel drawn to, since there is no possible way of seeing them all. I went to a session in which I was interested because the speaker was a prominent national figure on the scene. He began the session by stating that he was "not really in the mood to be here, but I made a commitment to doing the presentation, and I'll give it my best shot." This was his opening line?! Turned out almost all were not in the mood to listen to him either, and most (myself included) walked out shortly after.

It all begins at the beginning

It has often been said that you cannot *not* make a first impression. No matter what, you are going to make a first impression, whether it is good or bad. And your audience will decide in the first few minutes of your presentation which one that is. In fact, it has been well documented that the time you have to make a first impression is measured in seconds, not minutes. Therefore, how you start your presentation is crucial to the overall success of your presentation.

Let us offer some practical steps for starting a presentation.

Open with power!

At the beginning of your presentation, almost everyone is behind you. How many people do you know who wish to leave home, drive an hour, get herded into an unfamiliar room, and drink cold coffee so they can listen to a boring talk? The audience wants you to succeed. They really do. They are eager to listen to you. They are eager to learn. So give them every reason to continue to support you.

Instead of leading them through the table of contents of your speech or saying something predictable, open with a challenging statement. Open with a confrontational question. Get them involved right away. Make them think. Invite them to be a part of your seminar.

Kam has given several talks on corporate compliance for healthcare professionals and how these types of organizations can avoid running afoul of the law. His audiences are always polite but, knowing the subject matter, they are hardly enthusiastic about attending. Once again, pretty dry stuff.

A Story from Kam

The first time I gave a compliance presentation, I opened with "Today, we are going to be talking about corporate compliance and how your organization can comply with government regulations."

Pretty neat stuff, right? Had them beggin' for more, huh?

The second time I gave the presentation, I opened with, "How many people have been in jail… and would like to talk about it today?"

I am sure I could have come up with something better, but I guarantee you, the second opening did a better job of grabbing the attention of the audience. It began the critical process of building rapport with them.

Opening with power means pulling your audience in, either through questions, quotes, stories, or humor. All can be effective if properly done.

Memorize the first two to three minutes of your speech

This recommendation alone will instantly improve your presentation! Memorizing the first few minutes of your presentation will do several things:

1) It will allow you to plan your first few sentences, so you can ensure you open with power. Remember, you are going to be making a first impression. It's not good enough to just hope it happens. Plan for your first impression to be positive.

2) It will settle your nerves and eliminate the "fear factor." Even experienced speakers get nervous before a presentation. Memorizing the first few lines allows you to get into the flow of the presentation, and more quickly into your own comfort zone.

3) It will allow you to effectively convey the major points and goals of your presentation and decrease the odds that you will be misunderstood or stumble over a critical opening concept.

Jokes are for jokers

Many presenters like to tell a joke or two to settle the crowd, get them comfortable, and begin building commonalities between the audience and themselves. This has worked in many situations for many presenters. However, we have seen it fail more times than succeed.

Therefore, if you are not a good joke-teller, then don't open with a joke.

There are some gifted individuals who are good joke-tellers. Many of these people are professional comedians, and even they bomb every once in a while. However, if you ever listen to gifted presenters open with a joke, they rarely tell one-liner setup jokes like:

"An elephant walked into a bar and... "

Instead, professional comedians use what we call conversational humor.

"I was walking downtown the other day and entered a building that had a sign on the door that said 'No Dogs Allowed Except Seeing-Eye Dogs.' Now, who is going to read that sign? The dog or the person who is blind?"

They will usually masterfully expand this line of thought, following their observations with other stupid signs before relating this concept of stupid signs with their main topic.

This type of humor is much more effective and relevant to the audience and flows smoothly from one topic to another. If you can pull this off, fantastic. Congratulations. You are in a very select group of individuals.

The humorous story must relate to the main topic if you are going to open with a joke. If you cannot tie in your joke to the topic you are presenting, better to forgo telling the joke and just move on with your presentation.

Finally, if you are not good at telling jokes or being humorous, it is not a big deal. There are many different powerful ways to open your talk. But, please, if you are not a natural comedian, don't ruin your talk by trying to be one.

Avoid items that are not part of your central theme

There are two categories of items that don't belong anywhere near your presentation. First are those subjects about which nobody really cares. Remember, you are to open with power.

Why do people use the crucial first two minutes of their presentation telling people where the restrooms are or where to pick up copies of the handout or where there is more seating? In fact, these are items that should have been done prior to you taking center stage.

In the real world, there are times when you are the only one to communicate these informational sorts of things. When we have to perform these housekeeping items ourselves, we walk up in front of the audience, tell them what needs to be said, and then say they have two minutes before the presentation starts to get that last cup of coffee. That way, when we begin our presentation, we focus on our opening and the audience can focus on us.

The second category is items that, well, don't belong in any presentation, ever; but for some reason always seem to be included at the beginning. The biggest of these are apologies.

Rarely do we equate apologies with the concept of opening with power. However, for some unknown reasons, presenters across America see the need to apologize to their audiences. And for the same unknown reason, when people apologize, they think that the proper place to do it is at the beginning of their presentation.

We have heard so many ridiculous apologies at the beginning of presentations that we are now categorizing them. We have:

"I am not very good, so why don't you all leave now" apologies:

"I am sorry you have to listen to me today."
"I am going to open with a joke now."
"The topic for today is so big that there is no way I can do it justice, but... "

The "I don't know what I am doing up here" apologies:

"The regulations are still tentative, so this could all change by tomorrow."
"I am really not comfortable talking about this topic."
"This is the first time I have spoken on this topic."
"You know, I am far from an expert on this topic."

A favorite apology in this section was one Kam heard in a breakout session at a national convention. The speaker initially stumbled through a one-liner joke and then actually began her presentation by saying "Well... here it goes." (And believe me, whenever she said to her audience "Here it goes," well... there they went.)

The "I am unprepared, a little frazzled, and disorganized but please forgive me" apologies:

"I am sorry the handouts are not in order."
"I had a bunch of material that I meant to bring with me, but I forget it back at the office."
"Oh, I had this great slide to show you, but I could not find it."
"I am sorry that I did not have adequate time to prepare for this speech."
"There is this really good story about this subject, but I can't remember it."

And finally, general apologies that we all can do without:

"I'm sorry you can't read my PowerPoint slides but… "
"Can everyone hear me without the microphone?"

Apologies may be helpful in your personal life, like when you forget about your spouse's birthday, but let's keep them there. Here is a not-so-little secret: Nobody really cares about your apology when you are presenting. In general, it is best to skip over any apologies you may think you need to say and move on with your presentation.

COACHING POINTS

✓ Open with power.
✓ You don't get a second chance to make a first impression.
✓ Memorize the first two to four minutes of your presentation and your last one to two minutes.
✓ Get the audience involved from the start.
✓ Use jokes appropriately, in both content and style.
✓ Eliminate housekeeping items and apologies from content.
✓ Relate the opening and closing of your talk directly to your theme.

CHAPTER 6
HOW TO END YOUR
PRESENTATION

"It ain't over til the fat lady sings."

Now that we have covered how to begin your presentation, let's take a look at how to end on a high note.

A Story from Dan

> I went to hear Lou Holtz, the famous football coach, speak at a national seminar that featured several big-name people from several different industries. After a forty-five-minute part-motivational, part-hilarious presentation, he ended by talking about one game and motivating his team during a pre-game talk. He had to get them fired up to play against a team that was bigger, stronger, faster, and just better than they were. His team was scared and he joked that the last eleven players out of the locker room were going to start the game. The fans and announcers never saw a team bust out of the locker room and onto the field like that before. In fact, it scared the opponents as well. Long story short, they went on to win the game. His closing message to his pre-game talk was to go out there and have confidence in yourself, knock the walls down, and blow away the competition even when you think they are better than you. A great ending to a terrific story that sent his players on the field with a strong sense of action and purpose.

The end of your presentation is as critical as its beginning. Too often, even experienced presenters fail to capitalize on this most important element in their presentation. They allow time to slip on by and then hurry their closing. Or worse, they allow the presentation to wither to a slow death because the last slide has come up on the screen and nobody has anything left to say. Just like in your opening, where you planned to make a first impression, you will also want to plan to leave a lasting impression.

Memorize your closing

A closing lasts no more than a minute or two, and should be easily remembered. It is important to memorize your closing for several reasons, but let us list three:

First, since a lasting impression is so important, you don't want to forget about or leave to chance the life-changing and prophetic words you want to say. Your words should be preplanned and easily retrieved.

Second, a prepared ending makes you look smart, or at least organized. It is the equivalent to the back cover of a book. Your presentation's ending puts everything you said into context, and provides closure to your message.

And third, if you do have a question and answer period at the end of your presentation, a prepared closing always allows you to end on an upbeat. It would be our recommendation that you never end with a question and answer period. Nothing is more anti-climatic than answering questions for one individual while everybody else sits around. In larger settings, people start to migrate out throughout a question–and-answer period. This is why we may take a question or two, but then we usually close, and *then* state that we will be available for questions after the conclusion.

Memorizing your closing has one final benefit. Read on.

Never, ever, ever exceed your time limit

We can't be more blunt. There is never a good reason to go over your allotted time.

For us, it is an issue of respect and purpose. Choose to respect your audience and their time. If you have managed your time so poorly that you have not covered what you need to, simply state that you wish you had more time and that you would be willing to discuss such topics after your presentation. It is rude to hold your audience hostage because you have more to say.

As for purpose, the entire reason you are presenting is most likely to communicate something. Therefore, good communication only works when you are effectively presenting and the audience is effectively listening. Whenever you exceed your allotted time, you may be effectively presenting, but we assure you, the audience is not effectively listening! Instead, they are counting down the seconds until they can leave. Communication has ceased, and so should you.

A Story from Kam

Several years ago, I was part of a joint presentation that was supposed to last for one hour. Each of the three speakers was to talk for about twenty minutes. I was batting clean-up. The presentation started about five minutes late, with the first speaker talking for twenty-five minutes. The second speaker also spoke for about twenty-five minutes. As the second speaker ended his section, I glanced at my watch, noting that there was only five minutes left before the top of the hour. I was steaming mad. I had worked hard to prepare for a twenty-minute presentation. Now what was I supposed to do?

I guess I could have "damned the torpedoes" and forged ahead. Instead, I walked calmly to the podium, summarized my section in about four minutes, and stated that if anybody had further questions, they could see me after we ended.

I also made a point to call my colleagues the next day to see how we could work around this in the future.

While it angered me to spend time preparing for a speech I was not able to give, going past the time limit for the session would not have done any of our team any good. The audience would not have listened attentively and they would have viewed me, not my colleagues, as the person holding them past the time limit.

The rule always holds: Never, ever exceed the time limit.

Memorizing your closing will assist you in coping with such time constraints. With your ninety-second close ready to go at any time, no matter where you are in your presentation, you can always present your closing and it will look as if you planned to end your presentation right where you did.

Therefore, end early and look like a genius.

COACHING POINTS

- ✓ Relate the opening and closing of your talk directly to your theme.
- ✓ Don't allow the question-and-answer period (if you have one) to be the last thing they hear.
- ✓ End with an upbeat closing remark.
- ✓ Memorize your closing.
- ✓ Leave a final impression.
- ✓ Always end on time.

CHAPTER 7
ORGANIZING YOUR
PRESENTATION

Making your list, checking it twice.

There are many successful ways to organize a speech that will result in effectively communicating with your audience. First and foremost, you need to organize your presentation in a way you feel comfortable, and in a way that accentuates your personal skills and presentational style.

However, there are some basic principles that may help you in this process.

A Story from Kam

I will never forget one presentation by a group of accountants. They were presenting the results of an annual salary survey and had a room full of willing listeners, eager to learn just where their own paycheck ranked with their peers. Unfortunately, it appeared that the presentation was organized by, well, a bunch of accountants. The presentation *was* very organized. The format was logical and the program made perfect sense — that is, to any other accountant. But to the non-accountant attendees, I think they were hoping for something else.

The one-hour presentation proceeded as follows:

First twenty minutes	Survey methodology
Middle twenty minutes	Data aggregation and grouping techniques
Last twenty minutes	Survey results

Does anybody see a problem with the order of the presentation? Of course you do. Why in the world would you bore your audience — an audience that was on the edge of their seats at the beginning of the session — with a discussion of survey methodology and aggregation techniques? All Mary Jane wanted to know was how her salary measured up to the survey.

How did the attendees who endured the first two segments feel by the time the presenters reached the last twenty minutes? Frustrated? Relieved? Irritated? Annoyed? Is this how you want your audience to feel?

Perhaps a better way to present a salary survey would be to discuss overall findings right up front and then present highlights based on what was and was not found in the study. And then maybe, if you have time, you could discuss the methodology behind the survey.

Big ideas and stops

When initially organizing your presentation, it is always a good idea to jot down your BIG IDEA(S).

What is the purpose of your presentation? What do you want to accomplish as a result of your presentation? What are the takeaways for the audience? These questions should guide you in deciding what your BIG IDEA should be. Generally, you should try to have one BIG IDEA for every twenty to thirty minutes you speak. However, we have seen many fifty-minute presentations where the speaker had only one BIG IDEA.

You are taking your audience on a journey, an adventure, and your BIG IDEA is the destination.

Once you know the purpose of your presentation and you have identified your BIG IDEA (your destination), create a road map that links each BIG IDEA together, with stops (stories, data, quotes, statistics, research, etc.) along the way. This road map should serve as your guide throughout the presentation and will help you stay on course.

The stops are the real guts of your presentation. Each stop is a mini-presentation. Just like a stop on a sightseeing tour, everybody gets off the bus to experience a new event at each location. Tour bus stops are multi-experiential, including sights, sounds, emotions, smell, and touch. So should your presentation be.

Stops are where detailed information is given and learning for the audience occurs. But don't fall prey — especially if you are an accountant, an engineer, or a coach — to the thought that the guts of the presentation take precedent over the BIG IDEA. How often have you heard a speaker say "If you don't remember anything else I said today, remember this: _____." Well, this blank should be, if the speaker is any good, the BIG IDEA!

Between the stops, you will need to insert transitional statements so you can move from one stop to the next without it being awkward. While the stops act like separate chapters in a book, the transitional statements link each chapter together. Of course, the overriding theme of the book correlates to the BIG IDEA.

At this point, your outline should look something like this:

1) Opening
2) Big Idea #1
   a) Stop
      i) Story
      ii) Data
   b) Stop
      i) Example
      ii) Data
   c) Stop
      i) Data
   d) Transitional statement

3) Big Idea #2
   a) Stop

       i) Story
   b) Stop
       i) Illustration
       ii) Research
   c) Transitional statement
4) Big Idea #3
   a) Stop
       i) Data
   b) Stop
       i) Story
       ii) Data
   c) Stop
       i) Data
   d) Stop
   e) Transitional statement
5) Big Idea #4
   a) Stop
       i) Story
       ii) Data
6) Planned close

Concept outline

Once you have your BIG IDEA(S), stops, and transitional statements, you need to decide on how you are going to remember your presentation. We usually write short presentations out word for word. A short presentation to us is less than five minutes. For anything longer than that, we will usually use a concept outline and identify several key words or phases for each concept.

To construct a concept outline, list out the BIG IDEA and then bulletpoint any stops. Next to each stop, list keywords, stories, jokes, etc. that you want to cover at that stop (remember, each stop is a mini-presentation). If you have a major point or important quote you want to make at a stop, it may be best to write this out. Typically, a major point takes no more than a sentence or two to articulate.

An Example from Kam

Not too long ago, I did a fifty-minute presentation to a group of hospital CEOs and CFOs on a new government regulation that was going into effect. While the topic was one with which I was very familiar, these regulations would be drastically new to my audience, so I needed to find some good points of interest knowing that government regulations can be tedious to explain and boring to listen to.

I have included my concept outline of this presentation in Appendix A as one example of how you may want to consider organizing your material. My keywords are highlighted in gray.

Using a concept outline, one can usually outline an entire speech on one piece of paper. As a general guideline, we suggest one concept page per half hour of talking.

Everyone is different, so the number of pages you use is not particularly important. However, the practice of identifying your stops and then listing key words and major points to be made at each stop, will allow you to focus less on each particular word, and instead concentrate on the overall delivery of your presentation.

Who cares?

Now that you have your presentation organized, go back through your material and for every stop, ask yourself these four questions:

1) Who cares?
2) What do I want the audience to remember?
3) How do I want the audience to feel?
4) What do I want the audience to do?

The "who cares?" question is simply to identify how this stop fits in with your overall theme and BIG IDEA. Too many times, presenters get off-point with real-life examples and stories or with detailed information that is only marginally related to the topic. They believe such points are important to the presentation, but in truth, nobody really cares about them, except the presenter.

If the answer to the "who cares?" question is "nobody," either delete this stop from your presentation or begin this stop with an explanation of *why* he or she should care about the facts.

The last three questions have everything to do with the overall effectiveness of your presentation. Do you ever wonder why some presentations last like "Chicken Soup for the Soul" and others are like cheap Chinese dinners that leave you hungry an hour after you have eaten?

That is because the chicken soup presentations made you remember the stops along the way and had you "feel" the impact of the message. In most presentations, this occurs not by accident, nor is it just magic that happens when the sun and the moon align. Such feelings are preplanned and are purposely crafted events. You can do this too!

Using your outline

Now that you have your presentation organized in a concept outline with a BIG IDEA, stops along the road with examples, and stories to highlight each stop and transitional statements to move from stop to stop, you are now ready to give your speech. However, please, do not read your presentation. That is why you have a concept outline. Believe us, your audience wants to have a conversation *with* you, not be lectured *by* you.

If you are using a concept outline, there is really nothing to read. Instead of sentences and paragraphs, you have bullet points and thoughts. Don't worry about every single word you say or get wrapped up in using just the right phrase. Most audiences are very forgiving if you stumble on your words or need to correct yourself. They are more interested in your tone and overall message.

This "do not read" policy especially applies to overhead slides. Overhead or PowerPoint slides should guide your audience through the presentation and give reinforcement for visual learners. While the slides may contain keywords that you repeat, nothing is worse than seeing a presenter turn his back to the audience and begin reading the slides out loud. If you are not presenting to a group of second graders, assume that your audience can read the slides. Why then repeat what they already know? Your slides should help the audience connect with the content of your speech. Reading the slides, except to emphasize an occasional point, is condescending to your audience, boring, and shows a general lack of preparedness on the speaker's behalf.

The only exception to this "do not read policy" may be for those very rare times when your speech will be published or scrutinized due to the setting or content. If you are speaking at a shareholders' meeting or running for political office, it's best to keep with the script.

COACHING POINTS

- ✓ Organize your presentation by considering your speaking style, the topic, and the audience.
- ✓ Focus on a few BIG IDEAS.
- ✓ Integrate creative stops to present details about the BIG IDEAS and transitional statements to move on to the next stop.
- ✓ Use a concept outline that will emphasize your BIG IDEAS.
- ✓ Ask yourself what the audience should walk away with.
- ✓ Never read your presentation to your audience.

Chapter 8
Storytelling

Once upon a time...

People love stories. Hollywood knows this all too well. They sell stories to the public through television and movies, and they make lots of money doing it. But don't worry; we don't have to be as good as Hollywood (on their good days) when we use stories in our presentations. We do, however, have to be good enough at using stories to make our presentations come to life.

A Story from Dan

Bruce Springsteen is an amazing entertainer. His music has been around for decades and he has a shelf full of awards for his musical contributions. Seeing him many times in concert over the years, I have learned that Bruce Springsteen is also a great storyteller. Each song has a story and he does an incredible job of allowing you to visualize the story before he performs it. He blends fact with humor, and that technique makes the song more powerful. He invites the audience in, and takes them along on his storytelling excursion. He makes you feel like you are a part of the songs, and you stay connected to him throughout the entire show. By doing this, he captures the audience's attention, and before you know it, you are singing along.

As a speaker, regardless of the topic, you never have the right to be boring. A way to ensure you are inspiring is to become a master storyteller. There are some basic concepts about storytelling that would be good to follow. Here are a few.

Paint the picture

Words to a master storyteller are like brushes to a painter. As a speaker, it is your job to paint a picture with your words. Therefore, be descriptive with your language. Let the audience imagine what you are describing, whether it is how you and your co-workers solved a big problem, or the "real" story of how you broke your arm. You may describe the setting, but be sure to describe people, the smells, the noise, and the activity, as well. People are fascinating – how they look (without making fun of them), how they act, how they react. What are they wearing that may tell us about their personality? Use rich words, without being too flowery. Like a good movie or book, describe the action and build the interest. Use twists. There are so many ways to make stories come to life.

Along with colorful descriptions, the approach you take to telling a story can make it real. Talk like you are speaking to your Uncle Fred or Max, your co-worker. Try to recount the experience as if you were sitting out on the back porch with your best friends, telling stories on each other. Some people suggest you make your whole presentation with this informal demeanor, and there may be some merit in that. But remember, when you are making a public speech, some "professionalism" may be appropriate.

However, where stories are concerned, the folksy, down-home, informal storytelling tone works great for many people. One last tip when telling folksy stories: Make it real by telling one person the story, and let the others listen in. This technique allows everyone to feel like the story is for them.

A short list of things to remember when telling stories (or for that matter, whenever you are speaking):

- Use images and word pictures.
- Use stories that everybody can relate to.
- Cite examples that draw people in.
- Use personal stories (these are always the best).
- Speak with passion and emotion.

Fitting the big picture

Make sure that the stories you use are applicable to the topic. Just like all the other elements of your presentation, from jokes to the big ideas, your story should have a relationship to what you are talking about. It makes no sense to spend time thinking up some brilliant or funny story to tell, and then, not use that story to make a clever point about the issue at hand. People may tell interesting stories about their crazed dog, nutty neighbor, or clueless boss, but if the stories don't add to the presentation, they are just a short distraction. You can be creative in how you relate a story to your topic, but just don't stretch it too far.

Movies are two hours long, but...

Keep your stories relatively short. This is extremely important. Stories should last no more than a couple of minutes. Less than a minute is great. Create a scene for them in their minds. Make a point. Move on. The audience is with you.

When a story is too long, some will start to wonder what the main topic is. Some will just lose interest if the story does not resolve quickly. And some will wonder if the speaker is more interested in talking about himself than in the topic. People may also think that you maybe, just maybe, don't have anything really important to tell them. Even though they are technically listening, your audience may tune you out or not take you seriously. This is not good.

Where to find stories

The good news, as a presenter, is that stories are all around you. They are happening every day at work, at home, in the neighborhood, while driving, when walking the dog – pretty much everywhere. The wealth of resources from which you can find good stories is plentiful. Here are just a few:

Stories from history

Kind of like Paul Harvey's *The Rest of the Story*, people do enjoy hearing about the lives of famous people. And, like Harvey, it is fun and interesting not to reveal the main character of the story until the very end. Try using one of Harvey's stories (make sure to credit him afterward), or draw from your own reading and exposure to history.

Stories from pop culture – movies, books, etc.

Since so many people's lives revolve around pop culture, you may tell stories from popular movies, TV shows, or books. You may even tell stories from not-so-popular shows, and books that a few people may be familiar with but, as always, keep the tales interesting, lively, and appropriate to the topic. Referencing a story that is in the news or that is in a blockbuster movie is fine. We would not suggest retelling the story if most everyone knows it, but using the story as an analogy or to make a point can work well.

Stories from your life

If you want to tell stories that the audience does not know, tell a story from your own life. It may be a story from work that tells how you arrived at your conclusion. It may be a story from your personal life that helps describe a particular facet of your topic. Using people you know, including yourself, will make it real to you, help you be more comfortable with the story, and make you more personal to your audience. This is all good.

But please, don't get carried away. Nothing is more frustrating than when a speaker gets way too detailed about his or her own experience or family, elaborating on things that have no direct bearing to the central theme. The next thing you know, you are looking at home video of his or her most recent vacation as he or she recants every small detail about the wonderful experience. It kind of reminds me of the time when one of our friends went to Paducah, Kentucky over college break and stopped in at a Burger King right off the interstate. He really ordered regular fries but they super-sized it for him by mistake. Some of the fries spilled over in the bag and he had fries all over the inside of the bag. Some of the fries were on top of the burger he ordered, while some of the fries had actually stuck to...

(Uh-oh, we're sorry. We accidentally started to tell a really boring story that nobody cares about. So, on to the next topic.)

Let's remember

To recap the most important point about stories: Use them! When you use them, make them short, real, and have a point to them. Relating a long story can cause you to lose the audience, unless, of course, it is a very interesting story. If it is not about having dinner with Arnold Schwarzenegger or Ted Turner, then it is not interesting. Therefore, keep it short. Stories should only be two minutes long at a maximum. Shorter would be better.

Make it real. Paint a picture of your conversation with the police officer who gave you your last ticket or the battle of Waterloo. Don't read it word for word, but speak like you would in a conversation with a friend.

As with all other elements of your talk, any story needs to relate to your topic and hopefully emphasize a certain point. A concise, meaningful story will tie in clearly with your topic, while a vague, unrelated story will have people wondering, "Nice story, but what did it have to do with his presentation?" If that happens, you have lost them.

In order to jump-start your creative thinking, in Appendix B, we have included a few examples of stories from movies and history that make good lessons for presenters. We emphasize that these are only a few, a very small sampling, an extremely minute number of the myriad of possibilities. Let your mind go. Reach back into your memory for any story you know. Research a little in your movie library or on the Internet. Make engaging connections for your audience to experience.

COACHING POINTS

✓ Use stories in your presentation.

✓ Be creative in your use of stories, using unique tales that are personal to you.

✓ Paint a picture for the audience to make them feel they are there with you in the story.

✓ Use a conversational tone when telling a story.

✓ Pull stories from different areas – history, your life, the news, etc.

✓ Make the stories genuine, short, and relevant to your topic.

Chapter 9
Make It Come
Alive with Props

"It's alive! It's alive!"

In movies, theater, and television, the mantra for making a scene effective is "Show, don't tell." The same is true in a presentation. The more visual the presenter can make his or her topic, the more interested the audience will be.

A Story from Rick

We are all familiar with the process in which designers draw up plans and write out specs; then they hand them off to others, who construct the product, whether that be a building, road, bridge, factory, automobile, or a newfangled ballpoint pen.

When giving a talk on the different perspectives held by designers and construction personnel regarding how a project should be built, I used props to make a clear point. Actually, this is an example of using a story from history and props together.

I was trying to explain that there needs to be increased communication between the two worlds of design and construction. I used a story I had heard about Thomas Jefferson. "When Thomas Jefferson read his Bible, he sometimes ran across verses he didn't agree with or didn't like. His solution was to cut them out, literally, with scissors. This holy book became known as the Jeffersonian Bible." At this point in my story, I pulled out a pair of scissors.

"Now, we have construction personnel who read plans and specifications and run across parts that they don't agree with or don't like. 'That can't be built this way,' they'll say. Their solution?" Holding up the scissors, I pulled out a sheet of paper I had copied from a specification book and started cutting. The result? I held up a spec book that had numerous holes that I had prepared in advance.

It made the point. Design and construction are two different entities with very different perspectives. To improve things, and to prevent having Jeffersonian plans and specs, we need some communication.

The use of props

Using visual props for a presentation is far more effective than describing the tool, machine, or whatever it is you are trying to talk about, or showing a photo of it.

Good

Better

Best

When a device or substance is small enough (i.e., there would be no need to widen the doorway of the meeting room to get it in), then bring it in and show the audience. If your area of expertise is nuclear waste or mutating germs, we wouldn't suggest the use of props, but realistically, most of our topics will be suitable for some prop.

Perhaps you deal with purely paper or computer-driven topics. While more difficult, you can make these topics visual if you put some extra thought into your presentation and think creatively.

If you are having difficulty trying to think of a prop because your topic is process oriented, try bringing in the end product based on your topic. You may write computer code, but bringing in reams of the printout of the program will not thrill the audience (unless they are paper salespeople). But, if you write computer code for a medical testing apparatus — like a personal glucose monitoring device — bring the monitor in to show them. While it may be your program that makes the device perform, this show-and-tell will help make the presentation more alive to the people listening.

Common items that people use every day often become suitable props.

Money is fundamental to many speaking topics. Thus, show money – real money, Monopoly money, or whatever you can lay your hands on. "Borrow" your kid's piggy bank. Ask the audience to "Show me the money!" by getting them to pull out their money. Make it interesting by taking some of it.

Kam makes presentations about finances to engaged couples. He asks them if they have money, and when they pull it out, he asks for a ten-dollar or twenty-dollar bill from one of the couples. Then he puts it in his pocket and continues on with his talk. This antic builds some humorous tension in the room while it serves to illustrate his big idea on the value, use, and handling of money. (He's also made a few dollars that way.)

Make your props relevant

Just like your stories, your props need to be relevant. Make sure the props relate directly to the topic at hand. This is even more of a necessity than with stories. If you use an end product as a prop, be sure that it is an end product that matches your topic. Don't pick something up and say, " Well, this is sort of like the laser disseminator we used for this experiment, only this one is smaller, a different color, uses less energy, and well actually, this isn't a laser disseminator anyway." (Wow, we're underwhelmed! This is *not* an effective use of props.)

A Story from Kam

Over the last several years, Kam and Earl Motzer — CEO at The James B. Haggin Memorial Hospital in Harrodsburg, Kentucky — have presented back-to-back at the same healthcare conference. This past year, Kam had to follow Earl, but Earl stole the show.

Earl's presentation discussed the advancing technologies in healthcare, what hospitals need to do to keep pace with changing technologies, and as a side note, why procedures that utilize these advanced technologies, such as colonoscopies, are extremely beneficial to the general population. At this point, Earl pulled out an endoscope (yes, the tool that is actually used by your doctor to perform a colonoscopy). As Earl walked around sharing several stories with the audience about the importance of routine colonoscopies (all the while holding the endoscope), he concluded his remarks on this subject by stating that if anybody was so inclined, he would be happy to perform a colonoscopy for them right after the meeting. Laughter flooded the room, but his point was made... and in rather a compelling manner, wouldn't you say?

Now remember, Earl is an administrator, not a physician. No one in the audience actually thought that Earl was going to perform a colonoscopy.

But with Earl standing in front of the audience holding the endoscope in his hand for all to see, what an awesome visual to drive home his point. Good story, and *great* use of a prop.

Let your mind loose

We have listed below some examples and ideas we have seen or used:

Examples
- Anthony Robbins (motivational speaker) – Pulled people from the audience and used them in his talk
- Bruce Wilkerson (from the organization *Walk through the Bible*) – Again, pulled people from the audience to sit in specific chairs on stage as part of his "Three Chairs" speech
- Tim Daggert (US gymnast and Olympian) – Brought his own pommel horse
- Zig Zigler (author and speaker) – Brought an old hand water pump on stage in talking about work ethic
- MADD (Mothers Against Drunk Driving) – Used a wrecked automobile as backdrop when speaking

Ideas
- Video clips
- Music (find a song or lyric that makes your point)
- Pictures, graphs, and charts
- Impromptu props (article of clothing, chairs, a lady's purse)
- Sports equipment (football, baseball mitt, trophies)
- Tools (hammer, wrench, screwdrivers, power saw, chainsaw – this should get their attention)
- Animals
- Costumes (we will just have to let you imagine what Kam looks like dressed up as a chef)

As with many of the topics in this book, be creative in your use of props. Make them relevant and have fun. This will help the audience pay attention and remember your presentation.

Coaching Points

✓ Use props when you can.
✓ Show, don't tell.
✓ Use items that are appropriate for your presentation.
✓ Use items from the audience.
✓ Props must be relevant to your topic.
✓ Be creative in the use of props.

Chapter 10
Know Your Audience

Guess who's coming to dinner?

It is extremely important to know and understand your audience. Are they peers? Corporate executives? College athletes? Are you speaking to men, women, or both? Unless you enjoy watching people casually escape the room as you speak, do your homework well in advance. With the luxury of the Internet, you can research almost any company, group, or program, and learn about their mission, values, goals, and objectives. These can impact your delivery. Whether you are talking to a group of business executives, college seniors getting ready to enter the working world, or a team of athletes preparing for a big game, it is crucial to understand your listeners, and to anticipate ways that your talk can speak to them in a beneficial manner.

Delivering a customized message means maintaining some degree of flexibility and creativity in your presentation. Your audience should feel like you are talking about them. They will be much more impressed with your presentation if you know certain facts about the group in general. It shows you have a sincere interest in who they are. Express that you know who they are and what they do. Your goal is to help them achieve their goals. If you prepare a canned speech and deliver it to any audience, it will ultimately fall on deaf ears. Have you ever listened to the acceptance speeches during the Academy Awards? As an example, you do not want to deliver the same speech to a group of teenagers about to enter college that you used on the National Women's Cancer Society. Understand the different demographics of your audience in advance, do some research on who they are, and tailor your presentation to add them into your message.

A Story from Dan

A dear old friend of mine was a great example of tailoring his speech to a particular audience. Mike Vogel was a former prisoner and survivor of the Holocaust, having spent more than two years in German concentration camps during WWII. Mike traveled the world delivering his message, making sure his audience understood the history and the crimes that took place. His undying mission was to inform groups of all kinds, making sure people would never forget that time during WWII. I went to see Mike many times over the years, and watched him deliver his message to numerous audiences.

Every time I saw Mike, his presentation was unique. I finally asked Mike how he customized his talk to each specific group. He explained to me that he had different variations depending on how much information he thought the audience could handle. For instance, when he told his story in front of high school students, he would give the PG-rated version, as he called it. If he was speaking to politicians or adults about his experience, he would give the R-rated version. The message was very clear and powerful, no matter to whom he was talking, but he included more or less detail based on who his audience was at the time. By customizing his message to each audience, Mike kept their attention. He purposely spoke at a level to which they could relate. Mike was always successful in his delivery, and his audience walked away knowing they had witnessed a special presentation. He didn't change the content, just the depth.

Likewise, giving a presentation to coaches about the specific techniques and strategies to help their players succeed in a particular sport will be quite different than the presentation you will give to the administrators who support the team in other off-the-field areas. Both talks will focus on how to create both successful team members and successful students, but since the role the two groups play is different, the presentations should be adjusted.

It is important to know whether you need to change the depth of your talk or the actual content of your presentation. This will be determined by your audience.

Where am I, again?

Dan will never forget going to a rock concert in the early '80s at which the band actually opened up with a loud "It's great to be here in Columbus!" Unfortunately, the show was in Indianapolis. You can imagine the crowd's response. Not the best way to start any show. While people stayed because their ticket had cost $50, the band had lost any connection they could've had with their audience.

While we can laugh at the band, all three of us have examples of this type of thing in more subtle ways. We have heard speakers who use the wrong name or abbreviation for their audience. For example, a presenter may say that he is happy to speak to this association, when everyone there works for a commission. Speakers are known to use the wrong abbreviations to agencies or associations, assuming the initials are derived directly from the full name. That is not always the case, and it is at these times that the person doing the talking loses all credibility with the audience, because the audience members are thinking, "This guy doesn't even know who we are."

A Thought and Story from Dan

As a coach, I give presentations to teenagers every day. Each team is unique, and over the years, I have learned what each team is capable of absorbing and how each member of the team responds to various messages. I use this information about these players as I prepare and give talks to them.

Such was the case recently when my high school soccer team was on the road to the state championship. They had set a goal early in the season, and they had worked incredibly hard to get to this point. I knew they needed to be motivated in a way they never had been before. They were a group of young men who, regardless of how focused they might be on their goal, by the nature of their age and inexperience, only saw life and opportunities in the short term. This audience of young kids was ripe for the story I was to present to them.

My fifth child was diagnosed with kidney cancer when he was sixteen months old. He will never be able to play most sports because of his condition. Thus, to emphasize what long-term opportunities and limitations might exist for them, I brought my son (who was four years old at the time), and sat him on my lap and painted a picture for them about opportunity. The boys sat silently as I tried to show them how important it was for them to take advantage of the opportunities they have in front of them. I let them know that they had been fortunate enough to get the opportunity to do something they loved and were skilled at, and that not taking advantage of the opportunity or doing less than their best should never be acceptable.

That team went on to play in the state championship that year and took advantage of every opportunity they had. The story I gave them, with my young son on my lap, really hit home with them, and helped them to see the big picture. Because I knew the unique characteristics of the individuals on the team, I was able to tailor the message to have the maximum impact on that team.

Knowing and understanding the background of your audience is imperative for a successful presentation.

Demographics

There are many, many characteristics of an audience that can be woven into a presentation to make it more effective for that group. Doing the research does not take a great deal of time, but it will pay off greatly. Talk to the session moderator or person who invited you to speak. Get on the Internet. Call a friend who knows the audience. Do your homework.

Here are some of the things you might want to know about your audience before your presentation:

- o Proper names
- o Line of work
- o What service they provide
- o What product they sell
- o Gender
- o Age
- o Goals and objectives
- o Values
- o Program and company mission

Listen to them, they're speaking!

As you become more comfortable in your own presentational style, you will also learn the art of "listening to your audience." We can't say we have ever actually stopped talking, perked up our ears, and tried to listen to the audience. But we are always getting feedback from them. Are they on the edge of their seats or slumped down in their chairs? Are they taking notes? Maintaining eye contact? Engaged... or just doing time? Are they following what we have to say? Or have we confused them? Worse yet, are they awake?

Based on the feedback one receives, it is important to try to adjust your presentation to meet the audience at their level. This can be difficult, and at times, a blow to one's ego.

A Story from Kam

Not too along ago, I was teaching an all-day seminar. I came to a new section of my presentation that, honestly, I did not adequately prepare. I thought I could pull it off, but after only a minute of discussing this new material, I knew I was in trouble. After five minutes, I had actually confused myself. I felt like a rookie speaker. Sweat formed on my brow. I paused, trying to figure out where to go next, and as I did so, I glanced up at the audience. My eyes slowly moved from my notes on the podium, past the microphone, and to the front first rows. My mind was not on what I was going to say next, but was engaged in a SOS prayer to GOD, asking that even though I was lost, the audience was still actively engaged and leaning on every word. This whole slow-motion process took about four seconds.

Unfortunately for me, God chose not to answer my prayer. I had lost the audience. If you have never lost an audience, they are a picture of all your greatest fears and look exactly what you are afraid they would look like. Most people were not engaged. Some folks were unabashedly looking around the room. Others are either openly sleeping, or in the process of dozing off. Of course, there are the three or four people, God bless their souls, who were trying to keep up with me, but they still had that glazed "What are you talking about?" look.

While I still had ten more minutes in this section of my talk, I had to change on the fly. I referred to the next section, a section that was very interactive in nature, and made some type of transitional statement such as, "Let's look at this next section because these two topics are closely related." Then I asked a question of the audience. Questions, whether rhetorical or not, are a great way to actively engage listeners.

While a lack of preparation did me in, listening to my audience allowed me to modify the direction I was headed, and to save myself and the presentation from total disaster.

The more you know about your audience, the better you can tailor your presentation. Some professionals advocate shaking hands with people as they come in as a way for you to get to know them and for them to get to know you. Others mingle throughout the audience prior to the start as a way of getting to know their audience. Both of these methods can be effective. However, if you don't know your audience until you arrive for your presentation, you have missed the point of this chapter.

COACHING POINTS

- ✓ Do research on the audience as part of your preparation for your talk. Know who they are and what they do.
- ✓ The more you know about your audience, the better you can relate your topic and have a better chance of connecting with them.
- ✓ Know the demographics of your audience (age, gender, line of work, etc.).
- ✓ Tailor your presentation so it specifically relates to this group.
- ✓ Listen to your audience and consider adjusting your talk based on that feedback.

CHAPTER 11
THE ACTIVE AUDIENCE

*"Put your right hand in,
take your right hand out..."*

An audience that is actively engaged in a presentation will always better remember the material and have a greater appreciation for the speaker.

A Story from Rick

In my collection of weird highway stories, I have a series of news items that involve strange spills that have occurred on various roads and highways around the world. A few of these include liquid chocolate, fortune cookies (the driver obviously did not read his that day), chili, 32,000 pounds of liver, 12 million bees, and — my personal favorite — seven tons of monkey waste from a zoo. If I am presenting to local highway supervisors or maintenance workers, I precede these stories by walking into the crowd and asking them for their own stories of interesting clean-ups they have experienced on their own roads. This helps them get more involved in the stories and in the session. Even if some don't share with everyone else, their story comes to mind, and they are actively listening. News stories prepared in advance could stand by themselves and start to lighten the atmosphere, but having the audience come up with their own stories engages them from the start and leads them to anticipate what is to come.

There are many different ways to get audience members involved in your presentation. Careful consideration to variables will help guide your decisions for interactive elements.

- What is the size of your audience?
- What are your comfort level and skills in an activity?
- What is the make-up of the audience (demographics, not cosmetics)?

Let's look at these few variables.

The size of the audience

The size of an audience will obviously dictate the type of participation activities that are feasible. For our purposes, we will define an audience as small if it has under 30 members, medium if between 30 and 100 members, and large, if over 100. There is no magic to these numbers, but they seem to work when considering interactive elements.

If you happen to be speaking to a crowd of a few hundred (a "large" audience), asking questions while walking out into the audience tends to be more difficult from a logistical standpoint. But for audiences between thirty and one hundred people, this technique is very effective. It will get you out from behind the podium, allow you to have more of a conversation with the attendees, and as a result, the audience is more likely to toss out answers to your questions. If there are fewer than thirty audience members, you can be even more interactive with them, having audience members sharing their views more freely, something which is much more difficult to control when the number of attendees increases over thirty or so. Therefore, as a general rule, you may, depending on other variables below and the topic itself, encourage more freedom in discussions with the audience as the size decreases.

For small and medium-sized audiences (fewer than 100), ask something other than yes/no questions. Such questions make for boring conversations. Ask questions that give your participants a chance to talk. Even better, ask questions that allow them to think and respond. This technique is especially effective if used a few times throughout your allotted time period.

For audiences with fewer than 100 people, interactive problem solving is often fun and effective. Rick recently attended a training session that used this method. Each table of six was given a set of objects to use for solving the problem. But with 100 people in the room, this definitely pushed the limits for an exercise of this type, and you could feel it. This type of breakout session typically works best for groups of thirty to sixty people.

For larger audiences, you may rely on asking questions and asking for a show of hands. But it is important to ask questions that will engage the audience and maybe give them some information. Many presenters ask questions that are answered in the positive by everyone who would raise their hands in agreement. "Are you with me? Let me see a show of hands!" or "How many agree genocide is bad?" or "Who here has ever eaten at a fast food restaurant?" Since pretty much everyone could answer "yes" to these, if they all respond, everyone would raise their hands. This really adds nothing to a presentation. Eventually, many people stop raising their hands.

A better technique with large audiences is to ask questions that will separate the crowd (not in an embarrassing way) and maybe give them some interesting things to think about.

"How many here have changed car insurance companies in the past three years?" About 25 percent raise their hands. "It looks like that is about one quarter of you, somewhat less than the national average rate of change. But for this demographic, that is about right."

"How many here know someone who has been in a car crash in the last year?" Eighty percent raise their hands. "If we work the numbers, one in thirty Americans will be in a crash of some sort every year. It is surprising that not more of you know at least someone who has been in a crash, unless maybe that someone is you."

Comfort level and skill

This is fairly self-explanatory. You can only do what you feel comfortable or capable of doing. Going out into the audience and having impromptu discussions with people is not for everyone. You will have to determine this for yourself. But we would encourage you to stretch yourself some. Try going beyond what you feel comfortable with once or twice. You can get better at different techniques and you may discover that you enjoy it. If not, pull back and continue at your comfort level. Our suggestion is to push yourself, for your sake and for the sake of your audience. But at any rate, implement some audience participation techniques.

The demographics of the audience

Knowing your audience is particularly important when deciding on which audience participation techniques to use. Are they people who tend to participate? Are they skewed in some personality trait? Concrete thinkers like engineers will not respond if you start asking them to do anything too touchy-feely. They just can't. So don't expect them to start sharing their feelings with other audience members. It just won't happen. Instead, use an activity that is interesting, but makes them think.

Likewise, a truly right-brained crowd, like artists, usually will shy away from thinking through problems. They'd much rather play; so use an interactive, fun activity to bring them on board.

COACHING POINTS

✓ Make your presentation interactive.
✓ Choose interactive elements for small, medium, and large audiences that fit your comfort level and demographics of the audience.
✓ Push yourself to try different activities in this area.

Chapter 12
Controlling Your
Environment

Am I crazy, or is it hot in here?

The issue is not whether you are an interior designer, process engineer, businessman, homemaker, computer graphics major, or closet techie. No matter how you slice it, you are responsible for your speaking environment. This not only includes making sure everything works, but also whether or not you have created the right feel for your audience, and whether or not the ambiance in the room is what you want.

Many speakers we have met take the responsibility of controlling their environment very seriously, because they know how important it is. In these next three chapters, we will discuss how to manage your environment, and what to do when things don't go exactly as planned.

A Story from Kam

I was on the program committee for an industry meeting, and was asked to introduce the speaker we had booked. One week prior to the meeting, I received a three page introduction that I was supposed to read "word-for-word." The three page intro not only had the speaker's background and qualifications listed, but also some relevant points and common interest items related to my group. But what really got me was that along side each phrase or paragraph I was to read were italicized instructions on *how* I was to read it, where I was to stand, any hand motions that I needed to include, the tone and voice inflection I was to use when I read it, and how the final paragraph was to crescendo as the speaker walked on stage. I thought the speaker had gone mad. And that was just the introduction!

And while even today, I still believe it was over the top for the setting, it is this type of attention to details that makes a speaker successful.

You and you alone are solely responsible for *everything* that happens during your presentation. Too hardcore? Maybe. Accurate? Absolutely!

If the overhead projector is not aligned, the PowerPoint slides are hard to read, the microphone cuts in and out, or the chairs in the room are too hard to sit in, your effectiveness as a presenter will be compromised. It is incumbent upon you to ensure that these items work properly and pass your inspection first — *before* the first guest arrives.

It is also important that you show up on time.

A Story from Dan

Several years ago, I had been invited to speak at a National Youth Sports Administrators convention in Gatlinburg, Tennessee. I decided to take advantage of this beautiful tourist city, and go several days early so I could sightsee a bit before my presentation. I could get a feel for the area and the room in which I would be presenting. Also, I could familiarize myself with the convention in general to add any last-minute details to my speech. I pride myself on never, ever being late for anything. I was there two days early. I checked everything I needed and was very familiar with the location and timing of my presentation.

After spending a day enjoying the city, it was time to go over my presentation one last time and head to the convention. It was a beautiful sunny day and everything seemed to be going very smoothly. I was completely and confidently prepared. I left my hotel room a good half hour before my talk was scheduled, and, with all my materials, I stepped into the elevator. Then, without any warning, just seconds later, as the elevator was between floors, it stopped and the entire compartment went completely black. No movement, no sound — nothing. The power had gone out in the entire building. I could hear people in the next elevator screaming and yelling for help. The only light I had was the light on my watch that was telling me how late I was going to be.

It took almost forty-five minutes before the hotel technicians could regain power to get us out of the elevator. I had just a two-minute walk to the convention and allowed myself ample set-up time as well. And, I came two days early to guarantee no problems would occur! Needless to say, I was fifteen minutes late for my presentation. These people had never met me before and knew not a thing about me. Nothing bothers me more than waiting for someone to be on time, so when I realized I was going to be late, I was in a panic, and I felt bad because these people had all paid to be there. When I finally arrived, I walked in as calmly as possible, explained what had happened to more than a few chuckles, and delivered the presentation. I had to shorten my talk by fifteen minutes so I would not exceed the time given me, as the next presenter was in waiting.

Fortunately, I had prepared well and knew what section of my speech to cut, but it just goes to show, you never know what can happen. Turns out a raccoon got into one of the electrical boxes and zapped the entire street. From that point on, I always try to stay on lower level floors and always use the stairs. Just in case.

It is equally important that you are not held hostage to the electronic equipment you are using. If you don't know how to use a piece of equipment, then either learn how to navigate it, or put someone in charge of the device who knows what they are doing. Nothing is more embarrassing for you, and frustrating for your audience, than to have you fiddle with your computer, projector, or some other electronic device as you try to get it to work.

While you can plan and prepare for many difficult environmental challenges, sometimes there is just no planning. Such was the case for Kam.

A Story from Kam

I arrived several hours early to prepare for a keynote presentation. I was very excited about this presentation because at this stage in my career, I had been given only a handful of "keynote" opportunities, and with a good group in attendances, I really wanted to do my best.

After asking for directions in the main lobby, I walked into a rather large banquet hall that was very distinguished. Column pillars lined the hall and there was a huge stage front and center with spotlights cast on this oversized "pulpit." Man, did it look impressive. Unfortunately, the rest of the room looked trashed, literally. It looked like a New Year's Eve party had just concluded. There was confetti all over the place with bottles and cups scattered around, all the chairs were in disarray, and some dinner tables still had plates with leftover food on them. It was truly a mess.

Thinking I had the wrong place, I searched for about fifteen minutes before going back to the lobby. I ended up at the conference center desk waiting for the facility director to arrive. After originally arriving two hours early, I now had about forty-five minutes before my presentation was to begin. When the conference director and the program chairman for that day's event finally got together, they discovered a mix-up had occurred. Much to the surprise of the program chairman, the facility director indicated that the main ballroom/banquet room had not been scheduled because there was no keynote presentation on the agenda. (Note to self: It is very troubling to a speaker to hear they have cancelled your speech before they have even heard you.)

Nevertheless, there *was* a keynote presentation scheduled, and I was it. The several hundred people who were walking through the doors seemed to have an expectation that they were only several minutes away from hearing a well-executed and thought-provoking presentation.

I waited in the wings as the facility director and the program chair conferred. It was decided that since all the people were already in the lobby area getting their last cup of coffee or donut, they would just bring in some extra chairs and have the presentation right there. They gave me an old hand-held microphone and had me walk through the crowd discussing my topic and asking questions. (I joked that it looked like I was Phil Donahue.)

Not exactly what I had in mind when I was preparing for the talk. Out with the PowerPoint slides, in with the handouts.

Should I have prepared for something like this? I don't think so. I am not sure I could have. However, it is always good to anticipate problems and to ask yourself when you are giving a presentation, what could go wrong? And then think through what you may want to do, just in case.

So, just how do you control your environment? Read on.

COACHING POINTS

✓ You are responsible for everything about your presentation, including the environment.

✓ Check everything to make sure it is working.

✓ Do not assume the equipment is set up properly; check it.

✓ Make sure the electronics work and everything about the room is good for learning.

✓ Be on time.

✓ If need be, improvise.

CHAPTER 13
T-MINUS TWO HOURS

"Houston, we shouldn't have a problem."

Your presentation does not start when you step up to the microphone after you are introduced. To do a good job, you obviously have to prepare your talk well in advance, but for the actual day on which you are presenting, the final preparation begins hours in advance.

Story from Kam

> Just recently, I was preparing for a presentation, and in my usual fashion, the evening before the presentation, I hooked up all my gizmos to my laptop computer, and then my computer to the LCD projector, to see if everything worked. Now, I have done this literally a hundred times, and usually never have any problems. However, this time, for some reason, my laptop and the LCD projector would not work together. Nothing on my computer would show on the screen, no matter what I did.

> Fortunately for me, the next day, I was able to borrow a co-worker's computer and the presentation went just fine. Turns out that we needed to download some port drivers for my computer before the LCD projector would work with my computer.

> I never had this happen before, and since I am technically challenged, I would have never figured it out if I had showed up for my presentation the next day and tried to get everything to work.

We have all been to presentations when things don't go quite as planned. These are the ones at which the audience members sit in stunned silence because the speaker was not prepared. Sometimes, these events are outside the control of the people "on stage" – construction noise on the roof or in the next room, loss of electricity, or sprinkler systems going off — we haven't seen this yet, but it would make for a great story. Most disturbances, however, are well within the control of the presenter, and with a little time invested in advance, most of these can be avoided. Here are several suggestions to help you prepare on presentation day.

Bring your presentation

This may sound simple, but we suggest that you actually bring your presentation with you. Now, we know what you're thinking. "Gee, guys. That's profound." But read on.

First, before you travel to the place for your talk, whether in town or out-of-town, check, double-check, and triple-check that you actually have the presentation. Unless the title of your presentation is, "How to Panic, Apologize, and Look Stupid for Thirty Minutes," this concept is fairly self-explanatory.

Rick has actually been to a presentation where the speaker forgot to bring the correct PowerPoint presentation, and did not realize it until he stepped on stage. Not the first impression this speaker was looking for.

Bring your props, handouts, etc. with you and set them in the appropriate places. Get these in place early so you won't have to worry about getting them there while the previous speaker is in the middle of his or her presentation.

Bring your presentation, such as a PowerPoint slide show, on at least three different mediums. Have it on your laptop, on CD, and on a jump/flash drive (and then put it on any other new technology that comes out between the time we write this book and the time you read it). New technologies are always coming out. Keep up with the new technologies by talking regularly with your company's IT personnel... or your teenager.

Get there early

Get to the actual room early. How early? We recommend two hours, but it really depends. You may be able to shorten this time to an hour if you have presented in this room before, with the same moderator, identical set-up, etc. But most of the time, we have found that people are presenting in a new room with new people in charge of the event. Since that is likely the case, we suggest getting there at least two hours in advance.

Check out the room

There are so many aspects of the room that are important for you to check on in advance. Walk around the room and get a feel for any unique characteristics. Sit down in several seats and check sight lines. Will everyone be able to see you where you will be standing? Will they be able to see your projection screen, if used? Will where you stand block anyone's view of the screen?

Stand where you will be speaking. Check the podium height, the microphone height, and the stage area around the podium, should you wish to walk out from behind the podium. There is nothing quite like going from famous to infamous by tripping over a power cord in front of one hundred people.

Check where you will be placing your laptop. Please don't try to set the laptop on the podium if there is not enough room. Depending on how you will advance the slides – remotely or from the laptop itself – practice hitting the proper button while talking to the audience.

Check out the lights. This may be more of a tech item, but it's a room thing, too. We have been to too many presentations (unfortunately, some of them were ours) where people have to fool around for a number of minutes with the lights to try to make sure people can read the screen. Check that ahead of time.

Choose the room temperature. In many of the evaluations we receive, there are more comments on the temperature of the room than the qual-

69

ity of the presentation. So, like it or not, we can only surmise that this is an important part of any presentation. This may involve working with the host or moderator of the event or the owners of the facility, but if it is too hot or cold, find that person that can set it right.

Also, with modern technology, most projectors are now capable of "daylight" projection and have the power of 2,500+ lumens. This means that you do not have to turn off all the lights in the room for everybody to see the screen. It always amazes us to see the after lunchtime speaker dim or turn off all the lights in the room so everyone can see the screen, only to discover that as the lights go down, so does everybody's heads.

Check the tech

It is important to meet any technical support person who is covering the conference or training. These individuals are extremely helpful people to know. We have found most of them to be quite pleasant and ready to assist the speaker. They usually know what you need, even if they often speak in the language of a techie.

Talk to the tech person about the microphone – how to use it, how to clip it on, how to keep it from making that nasty SSCCCCCTTTCCCCHH sound as you're putting it on. Ask about the laptop connection. Who will be getting your presentation on the screen (particularly if there is someone else speaking ahead of you)? Make sure you understand how to advance the slides, how to turn off the projection when you want, etc.

Once you get your presentation loaded and up on the screen, then go through the first few slides. Get a feel of how you are going to advance the slides. Different set-ups have different quirks and procedures, particularly when it comes to remotes for the laptop and projector.

If you are using props of any kind, place them where you want them and practice pulling them out. Run through how you plan to show them. If you have a video, make sure it can run on the system — and will work well. The more at ease you feel about details like this, the smoother the presentation will go.

Meet the moderator

Someone will undoubtedly be introducing you. Meet this person and ask them how things will proceed. Check the amount of time you have. Check the schedule of events. Make sure this individual feels comfortable introducing you with the advance information you sent.

Many moderators, particularly of sessions with multiple speakers, will have a particular way they wish to handle questions. Ask them how this will be done. If, as we have suggested, you have an idea on how to take questions and then end with power, work that out with the moderator.

Double-check everything

Now, do it all again. All right, you don't have to introduce yourself to the technical assistance person or the moderator again. They would consider that odd. But make sure everything else is working.

Appendix C is a good, concise list of things to check in the two hours before your presentation.

COACHING POINTS

✓ Bring your presentation in a few different media.
✓ Get to the site early.
✓ Take a walk around the room, and become comfortable with where you will be speaking.
✓ Get to know the tech person and let him or her help you walk through the equipment check.
✓ Make sure the moderator introduces you properly.
✓ Check and recheck *everything*.

CHAPTER 14
WHEN THINGS DON'T
GO RIGHT

We interrupt this speech...

When you have given enough presentations, you begin to think you have seen it all. Of course, "pride cometh before the fall."

A Story from Kam

Several years ago, I was giving many back-to-back seminars on a healthcare topic. It was pretty boring stuff. I was presenting for the third day in a row to a totally new group of wide-eyed and anxious attendees. Things were humming along pretty much as I planned. Even though it was the third day in a row, I had arrived at the seminar venue two hours early to check my equipment and microphone, and to make sure the room was properly arranged. What could possibly go wrong?

Midway through the morning, the hotel fire alarm went off for about thirty seconds. It was loud! However, nobody seemed to panic. When the alarm stopped, I made some lame comments regarding how "hot" the topic was and everybody had a good laugh. We got back to work.

Not five minutes later, the alarm went off again. This time, it lasted for about two minutes. It was so loud that I did not even think of talking over it — and worse, it was painful to the ears. When the alarm stopped the second time, nobody in the room was in the mood for any of my glib remarks, which was good, because I did not have any. We *tried* to get back to work.

72

For some, two fire alarms in five minutes was cause for real concern. While I was personally trying to ignore the alarms because it was causing havoc with my presentation, maybe the hotel was really on fire! To ease fears, one of the seminar planners was quickly dispatched to make sure the hotel was not actually on fire.

I am sure you are way ahead of me now. Two or three minutes later, the alarm sounded again. At this point, I was irritated. Scanning the audience, it was clear that their thoughts were on the loud noise and not on the stupendous points I was trying to make. Communication had ceased! What was I supposed to do now?

Believe it or not, I had actually planned for a situation something like this. Since the seminar was a day-long session, I had always thought that if anything really strange occurred, I was going to do the most rational thing possible – give them a break!! In fact, giving your audience a break will work almost any time you are in trouble. "He gave me too many breaks" has not once appeared on my evaluation forms.

So, I announced a break while making another lame comment about filling up your glass of water in case you may need to put out a fire.

Could I have handled this annoyance in a different way? Yes. I could have continued to ignore the sound, or asked everyone to stay in their seats while we checked out the alarm. However, the overwhelming factor was that I had lost the audience. I needed to do something until they could refocus their attention and maybe listen to what I had to say.

It is amazing to us just how often things don't go as planned. Lights go out. Projectors don't work. Interruptions occur. Stuff is going to happen.

Knowing this, you, as the presenter, must think ahead and have a backup plan, just in case.

Expecting the unexpected

Here are several suggestions that may help you in preparing for those unexpected moments:

1. Plan ahead.

    So, just how do you plan ahead for problems that you can't anticipate? Well, there are two types of problems. The first type is problems that are within your control. These include most technical issues (microphone goes out, computer hook-up fails, remote control does not work, room is too dark, etc.), room set-up not conducive to your presentation, room too hot, room too cold, handouts sent in advance that are not organized properly, etc. These problems must be anticipated. Be proactive to ensure that they do not disrupt your talk.

    The second type of problems is those that are difficult to anticipate, almost never happen, and are really not within your control. Nevertheless, you still need to be prepared for these kinds of situations on a broad basis.

    Therefore, prior to your presentation, think about what could go wrong, what may not work, and then develop some type of contingency plan(s). Creative thinking and a little flexibility can go a long way.

    Some examples include:

    *   Have an easel and paper available should the power go off or computer fail.

- Know you can always give them a break should the circumstances demand. Don't be afraid to call a time out.
- Carry extra supplies with you (power cord, batteries, markers that work, etc.).
- Bring a spare shirt or blouse should you need it.

2. Capture the moment.

For those truly unexpected, out-of-your-control problems, make the most of a bad situation. In Kam's story about the fire alarm, no one was going to blame him for the alarm going off and disrupting the seminar. In fact, he, along with everybody else, was in the same situation. However, what a great opportunity as a speaker to "make a memory," either good or bad.

The best way of making a positive memory is not to become flustered or overly concerned about the problem. Rather, remain calm, relax, and try to understand the mood of your audience, even if this means the joke's going to be on you.

One note of caution: These situations often lead to "speaking off the cuff" or ad-libbing. This can be dangerous. Having never anticipated such a problem or practiced what to say, some words can be inappropriate, out of place — or both. To prevent saying something you may regret, remain calm, take a deep breath, and think before you speak.

3. Humor is the best medicine.

The pressure of almost any situation can be released with effective and well-placed humor. While it is difficult to plan "funny" comments, not taking yourself too seriously is a start.

In fact, if the interruption is truly something that is out of the ordinary, odds are that there is humor somewhere in the situation.

Also, it may be helpful to have a few light-hearted lines ready to go at all times in case there is a major disruption. These can range from strange comments your dad or high school physics teacher had to say to off-beat stories from history. Do you know that the singer Frank Sinatra was (in part) responsible for having the Internal Revenue Service create a new income tax that affects millions of Americans today? Well, if the lights go out during one of our presentations, you may just hear the story.

4. Know what lines of communication are available if something does go wrong.

Should a problem occur, the best way to get back on track is to resolve the issue, and quickly. This usually means enlisting the help of the onsite coordinator who is more familiar with the local set-up and can quickly navigate to find an acceptable solution.

Most often, if you are like us, you are the speaker, planner, coordinator, cleaner-upper, and refreshment man. Knowing this in advance, it is best to identify a co-worker or buddy who can assist you if things don't go as planned.

We can hardly wait to hear all your stories about what's gone wrong in your presentations.

COACHING POINTS

✓ Even with all the planning and checking you *will* do, know that things, at times, still go wrong.
✓ Plan for the unexpected.
✓ Remain calm.
✓ When things go wrong, adjust your talk, and work hard not to lose your audience.
✓ Use humor to put people at ease.
✓ Give the audience "break time" if a condition prevents an environment conducive to learning.

CHAPTER 15
STAGE PRESENCE

"All the world is a stage."

Have you ever watched the President of the United States deliver his annual State of the Union Address? Talk about your entrance.

Every January, the President of the United States reports on the status of the country in a nationally televised State of the Union Address. As written in the United States Constitution, the President is to inform Congress from time to time about issues he has judged to be "necessary and expedient."

The President typically gives this address to a joint session of the U.S. Congress (the House of Representatives and the Senate) in the House of Representatives' chambers.

The opening procedure is quite chilling. The U.S. House of Representatives' Sergeant at Arms, standing in front of a closed door, ceremoniously calls out "Mr. Speaker, the President of the United States." The doors swing open as the President enters the chamber. People begin to clap with a standing ovation to follow. A faint "Hail to the Chief" montage plays in the background as the President slowly makes his way to the podium, stopping every step to be greeted by well-wishers who shake his hand and pat him on the back. It takes several minutes for him to walk the short fifty feet to the podium among the hoots and hollers from a crowd of supporters. The first two rows of the chamber are filled with members of the Joint Chiefs of Staff, the justices of the Supreme Court, and members of the President's cabinet (all of whom the President appointed), who continue to stand and applaud for several embarrassing long minutes until the President insists that they sit down.

We don't know about you, but we rarely walk into our own conference rooms amid that type of reception. However, when you take the "stage" for your presentation, you'd better be prepared to own the audience.

The two main tools

As a speaker, you have two main tools to use when it comes to stage presence – your body and your voice.

Body language is extremely important in your presentation. It is so important that we will examine it more closely in the next chapter.

Voice tone and projection are other key factors. This is even more important if there is not a microphone for your speech. Projecting the sound over the entire audience is vital. After all, they came to hear you talk. Make sure they can hear you. Nothing is worse than listening to a monotone speech that puts an audience to sleep. You may have to fight over sounds like heating and cooling vents or outside noises that make it difficult to hear. On the athletic field, there are always distracting noises such as lawn mowers, wind, cars, construction trucks, sirens, and chatter that make it difficult to hear. Keep in mind that there is a difference between projecting a strong voice and screaming. But make sure your audience can hear you. Sometimes the microphone and the sound system may be too loud. Be sure you check that too.

Also, varying your pitch and rhythm will effectively engage your audience and allow you to emphasize different aspects of your presentation. A strong cadence, an up-tempo section, or a strategically placed "pregnant pause" can all serve to augment the tone of your presentation.

Don't curb your enthusiasm

Present with energy that is realistic and sincere. Don't try to give a cheerleading presentation; it will come off as phony. Rather, deliver with natural enthusiasm because you believe in the message you are delivering. If you are not interested in what you have to say, your audience won't be either. Most audiences can tell whether you are sincere or not. Don't think they can't. Your audience is very smart. In other words, don't try to fake sincerity.

Can I hide behind the podium?

Make every effort to stand in front of your audience by using a hand-held or wireless microphone. This style will help relax the audience and will be a little less formal than the podium speech. Presenting in this format is an easier way to express yourself and make it feel like you are delivering a more natural presentation. Standing freely takes practice and preparation to deliver, but it will always come across well if it is done properly.

If a podium is the only option, be sure to make strong eye contact with your audience on a regular basis. Do not read your presentation or stare at your notes the entire time. You will lose the connection with them. After all, you are "up there" and your audience is not. Be sure to make them feel like they are a part of your presentation.

A Story from Dan

I delivered a speech to a group of young baseball players at an opening-day ceremony one year. About 500 players, coaches, and parents were in attendance. It was outside at the baseball field, and the host failed to give me a microphone. With all the outdoor noises going on and the wind blowing, I had to find a creative way to get myself in a position for the audience to hear me. I gathered all of them in a circle around me, made them sit so they all could see me, and rotated my presentation in a continuous circle so they could all hear me. I had to talk very loudly and it was not the best way to present, but I did what I had to do to make it work. I was upset with the people who had coordinated the presentation, who put me in an unprofessional position, but ultimately, the audience doesn't blame the committee. They only judge *you* and the presentation itself. Sometimes, you just have to improvise and do the best you can with what you have.

Whether someone else is introducing you or you will be introducing yourself, walk in with confidence and present yourself with a strong first impression. Introduce yourself and get right into what you are presenting. You display confidence by three things: 1) being prepared; 2) experience; and 3) knowing your strengths. Like the old saying, you never get a second chance to make a good first impression, so make it a good one.

COACHING POINTS

✓ Present with energy.
✓ Be sincere in your enthusiasm. Fake, insincere enthusiasm is easy to identify.
✓ Make good eye contact with your audience.
✓ Know your strengths.
✓ Present with a wireless microphone when possible.
✓ Use strong voice projection.
✓ Be flexible and creative with what you are given.

Chapter 16
Body Language

Okay, what do I do with my hands?

Understanding your strengths and weaknesses when it comes to your own body is key to delivering a solid speech. Walking freely with a wireless microphone also puts your audience at ease and leaves the impression of a more personable delivery. That doesn't mean run around like Jerry Springer, but move slowly and interact with the audience as you deliver your message. Obviously, this depends on the size of the room and the size of your audience, and on how well you know your message.

Use your hands appropriately. You can put your hands in your pockets, fold them over each other, or place them behind your back. Your hands will come into play naturally as you present your speech. Just don't let them be a distraction to your presentation through jerky movements or disruptive repetitive gestures.

An Observation from Dan

I was at a presentation where the presenter kept sniffling and wiping his nose with his hand. It was not only distracting, but he would then wipe his hand on his pants. The poor guy had a really bad cold or allergy going on, but his mannerism was not appropriate behavior while presenting. He probably didn't even realize he was doing it. I don't even remember what this guy talked about. It completely distracted the audience from his message.

When you get in front of an audience, personal habits can become visible. Be mindful not to let these behaviors become a distraction. Remember, everybody in the audience has their eyes on you. Once you understand this, you will pay more attention to your presentation behaviors. Video-taping one of your presentations will allow you to critique your behavior and improve upon it before your next presentation.

Don't take it, or give it, sitting down

Generally speaking, choose to stand for presentations whenever appropriate. When the audience is sitting and you are standing, you gain a positional edge. Do you ever watch a late-night talk show like David Letterman or Jay Leno? Have you noticed the host's chair is considerably higher than the couch where guests sit? This gives the visual effect that they are confident and in control. You are aiming for that same effect when presenting. Standing is the best option to accomplish this. If you are on a platform or stage, that is even better. Sitting to present is generally reserved for very personal or casual presentations. However, this can be used to your advantage whenever you want to make your presentation a little less formal and appear to be more intimate with a crowd.

You can also rearrange how the room is configured, in order to allow yourself the freedom to move about. Based on your individual style, this may allow you to have a more intimate connection with your audience. School teachers and university professors use this approach on a regular basis, creating a close-knit environment for learning.

Standing tall using good posture is a key factor in presenting a style of confidence. You don't need to stick your chest out like Superman, but a strong posture helps secure a confident delivery.

A word on facials

Facial expressions are also very important, especially if you have a question-and-answer session at the end of your presentation. How you react and respond to your audience, not only by answering their questions, but also how you express yourself non-verbally becomes part of your interaction. There are many looks you can give that may send a different message than you would like. For instance, you may have a puzzled look, a surprised look, a look of disagreement, or a look of sarcasm — sometimes without realizing it — in response to your audience. These expressions send loud and clear messages to your audience. Be careful to send the one that you want.

COACHING POINTS

✓ Know your body and realize the importance of your body gestures.

✓ Stand and walk with confidence.

✓ Adjust the room ahead of time allowing you to move about freely and deliver a natural discussion.

✓ Let your hands move naturally.

✓ Avoid embarrassing personal mannerisms.

✓ Watch your facial expressions.

CHAPTER 17
DRESS THE PART

Yes, what you wear matters.

The way you are dressed will either distract from or subtly support the real purpose of the presentation. You want to have these comments being generated inside the minds of the audience:

> "What an interesting point. I've never looked at it that way before."
> "How can I use this information in my job?"
> "My fellow employees should hear this."

You do not want the following bouncing around in their heads:

> "Why is he dressed like a high school student?"
> "That dress is so early '90s."
> "Does this poor man need more money for clothes? Should we take up a collection?"

A Story from Rick

When I was in college, there was one professor who was often mistaken by new students for a janitor. Many professors don't dress in coats and ties, but at least they understand the unspoken dress code. Not this one. He was often overlooked in his flannel shirt and older khakis with the dirt stains pressed into them. This was not someone who people would take seriously explaining intricate details about science. I don't have anything against custodians. They perform important services. It's just that I don't want them teaching me physics.

Right or wrong, our society links our roles with the way we dress. Audiences give initial credibility to someone based on what he or she wears. Don't give your audience a reason to discount you.

The reason for proper dress

The real problem with dressing inappropriately is that it will take away from the message. Both how well we present our message and how we look doing it affects how well the listener will pay attention to it. While our speaking style should supplement and add to the presentation, our attire should not be a distraction from the main purpose of the presentation. The way we dress should not be distracting to the audience.

So, how should we dress?

We have often heard that if you are making a professional presentation, you should always dress in business attire – coat and tie for the men, dress or business suit for the women. But we have been in many settings where that would be a turnoff for the audience.

Our thought on this is that there is a scale or spectrum of dress codes for both men and women:

The Spectrum of Dress

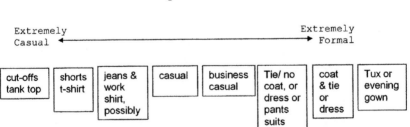

cut-offs tank top	shorts t-shirt	jeans & work shirt, possibly	casual	business casual	Tie/ no coat, or dress or pants suits	coat & tie or dress	Tux or evening gown

Extremely Casual ←——————————————→ Extremely Formal

Here's our theory: You should aim to dress one step "above" the majority of the audience. This involves (Have we mentioned this before?) knowing your audience.

Dressing below the audience obviously presents difficulties. Professionals who are dressed at least in ties have difficulty learning from a person who is dressed in jeans or wearing a T-shirt. But the opposite is also the case.

A Thought from Rick

I have spoken many times to people in highway construction or maintenance work. Let me explain one thing about most of the people in these professions: They don't dress any nicer than their work clothes. There's certainly nothing wrong with this. In fact, it is relatively freeing. But if I went to speak to them and stood up in a coat and tie, or even in a tie and no coat, I would have lost them before I even started. Dress in a manner that is professional, but appropriate to your audience.

We have identified several different levels between "casual," "business casual," and "tie, no coat" or "dress" because there does seem to be some debate about what "business casual" really is. Depending on your definition, you can remove a box or combine it with the box to the right or to the left.

The only exception to dressing at or slightly "above" the audience is if you are trying to make a point with wardrobe. You may wear formal attire to a "business casual" speech if you are representing a group that is known for this type of dress, or you may wear extremely informal clothes if you need to convey a message about people who dress like that. But if you vary from the basic principle, make sure it is part of a well-thought-out presentation package. In other words, don't be like the kids who color their hair purple because they are trying to "make a statement" and then get offended when people stare at them.

COACHING POINTS

✓ Dress slightly above the listeners' attire.
✓ Don't distract the audience from listening to you by dressing at the wrong level.
✓ Be sure what you are wearing is appropriate and professional for that setting.

CHAPTER 18
WORKING WITH POWERPOINT

Danger! Slides Ahead!

Studies have shown that 87 percent of presentations in a professional setting use Microsoft PowerPoint or a similar program. Okay, we made that number up. But based on our experience, it should be close. A presenter's ability to use PowerPoint to his or her advantage will make a huge difference in the quality of the talk. Here are a few suggestions.

A Story from Rick

I was in a video conference recently, with offices dialing in nationwide. The central office had a lineup of speakers, each talking about what was new in his or her area.

The first speaker did quite well, speaking clearly and showing clean, easily read, and understandable PowerPoint slides. The next two speakers lost the audience. Neither speaker had energy or passion. Their worst offense, however, was that a high percentage of these guys' PowerPoint slides were unreadable. They were packed with words. No one in any office around the country could read them. People in my office started talking to each other and paid little attention to the presenters' pitiful droning. While this behavior is not typical for live audiences, when on a muted line, it became clear to me what a poor presentation, beginning with poor slides, will do.

Even though this was a slightly non-traditional setting for professional presentations, our world is moving in this direction. Almost all of the advice in this book also applies to "remote" presentations such as the one noted above.

Clean up your slides

It doesn't matter how many times professionals receive training on how to put together a proper PowerPoint presentation; the truth is that many PowerPoint slides are not designed properly. We know that almost every professional has heard that there are rules as to how many words should be on a slide. Maybe one uses a twenty-five-word rule, maybe a "six-by-six" rule (no more than six words on a line, no more than six lines), but all trainers have taught perfectly sane, intelligent professionals how to make a slide properly. And yet, we still see slides that look like this:

Powerful Presentation Pointers for Your PowerPoint Presentations:
1. Make sure to have all words spelled correctly. People don't like it when words are not spelled correctly.
2. Be sure to get only the important points on any given slide. Extraneous material will only distract the audience.
3. Do not use too many words on one slide. People will not or can not read a lot of words on one slide. Make it concise, simple and abbreviated. You can fill in the details with your spoken words.
4. Do not repeat yourself unless it is absolutely necessary.
5. Do not repeat yourself unless it is absolutely necessary.
6. Be certain that all words are readable. Smaller fonts may not be able to be read by audience members sitting further back than the second row! You don't want that to happen. Choose your font size wisely.

Remember – Brevity is the key. People need only to read what is necessary. Writing many, numerous and ubiquitous verbiage will only serve to alienate people and they won't take you seriously and they won't listen, let alone read everything that you have written. There is no need to place all the information on a PowerPoint slide where it will never be read and cause you will not be listened to. Don't do it. It makes no sense. So don't even try.

Right after showing a slide like this, the speaker says something like "I know you can't read this slide, but... " Now, if the speaker knows you can't read what is on the slide, why is he or she still going to talk about it?

Here's a small tip on how to improve your PowerPoint slide presentation if your slides look like the one above: DON'T USE THESE SLIDES! Never. Ever. We think we've made that clear enough.

Listen to what the "human factor" experts and psychologists recommend regarding the look of slides. (Generally, keep to no more than six lines per slide, six words per line.) Force yourself to go through your presentation and clean them up. Save the details for your published paper.

A Story from Rick

I hesitate to bring up yet another bad example from the engineering field, but engineers make their lack of presentation skills and training so obvious. I actually saw a presentation recently where half the slides were images. If they were photos of the project on which the engineering firm was working, that would have been great. I think there were a few of those, but what I remember was a long series of images showing letter after letter of the correspondence between a city and the engineering firm hired by the state to design a road project and landscaping through the city. The discussion between the two was interesting. But the way it was displayed, through showing images of the actual letters back and forth, did not help the presenter's cause. His talk involved a lot of statements like, "And here is the letter in which we suggested a certain landscaping scheme. Here is the letter that the city sent back to us asking that we include planters that fit in with their historic theme. We then sent them this letter that explained..." We couldn't read the actual letters since the images were too small. But we didn't want to anyway. Unfortunately, the talk would have been very funny if it wasn't real.

Exceptions to busy-ness of slides

Of course, there are some exceptions to the rule of using simple slide designs. You may use a "busy" slide for two reasons. First, you sometimes want to show that there is some reasoning, that there are calculations behind the simpler statements in the presentation. For example, you could show a spreadsheet that gives an idea of the process of calculating a benefit-cost ratio. But don't expect the audience to read any part of the slide, and don't keep it up for longer than a few seconds. Using such a "busy" slide is for emphasis, not actual communication.

Second, you may show a "busy" table, then circle a part of it and zoom in on these few key numbers in the table. Again, the audience is not expected to read the entire table (and they won't, anyway), but it will give them a sense of where the important numbers fit in the grand scheme of things.

As a general rule, if your presentation is going to include technical data, charts, graphs, quotes from regulations, etc., it is better to bullet point the top concepts on your slide. This helps the audience to focus. Then provide a handout of the technical information. Heck, we have even used slides that read: "SEE PAGE 4 OF HANDOUT."

As Kam goes around to accounting conferences, he is always amused when the presenter crams an entire financial statement on one slide. The audience is full of accountants who LIVE to analyze such data — if only they could see it. The presenter has missed a valuable opportunity to connect with his audience. If only he had provided this information in a separate handout!

Working with your slides

Obviously, unless your slide is a few bullet points or a short quote, do not read it. Your listeners know how to read for themselves.

Also, do not face the screen as you flip through your slides. Computers are made with a toggle switch that will go between three settings: screen only, projector only, screen and projector together. Many people do not know this. If you don't know how to toggle your computer to the screen and projector together, find someone who can show you this. Then you can glance – notice the word is not *stare* – at the computer's screen while you still face the audience. There are also a number of other features within PowerPoint that can enhance your presentation (like pressing the function key and the letter "B" at the same time to take the screen to black).

If you ever observe Kam present, you will notice that he places the computer on a desk, table, or podium between himself and the audience. In that way, if he needs to refer to a slide, he can simply glance down to the computer screen while still facing his audience, never needing to turn around or otherwise divert the attention of his audience away from the point he is trying to make.

Exception to facing the audience

You may turn and face the screen only if you are using a laser pointer to focus the audience's attention to a particular location on the slide.

Bonus Points from Rick

I will sometimes look up at the projection screen and pretend I am surprised to see something in my presentation. For example, when pointing out the need for data, I will go to a slide with a photo of Data from *Star Trek: The Next Generation*. Then I will look at the screen in puzzlement or surprise and blame that on my son, the Trekkie who must have gotten onto my computer last night when I was going through the presentation and walked briefly away. It helps that I speak mostly to engineers, who have a higher Trekkie ratio than most professions.

To put it simply, for the love of all that is good in this world, make sure your slides are readable and use them to improve your presentation. Don't lose audiences because you have not paid attention to how your slides look or are used.

COACHING POINTS

✓ Don't put too much information on a slide.
✓ Save content for a handout.
✓ Clean up your slides.
✓ Make sure the slides are readable.
✓ Use state-of-the-art equipment when presenting and know how to use all the features.
✓ Don't read your slides.
✓ Face your audience, not your screen.

Chapter 19
Entertainment vs.
Education

"That's Entertainment!"

Occasionally, we have received comments on speaker evaluations that say: "tells too many stories"; "gets off topic with side issues that have little to do with the presentation"; and our favorite, "I don't want to hear any more stories, get to the point." These comments usually come from seminars that are rather technical in nature and are from well-intending individuals eager to learn (engineers, lawyers, accountants, executives, doctors). These people are linear thinkers who want to move on to the next subject and gain as much knowledge as possible. However, for every one of those comments, we get fifty-plus comments that encourage our style and indicate that an entertaining environment complements the learning process.

But how much is too much? Are we just entertaining the audience? What about content? What about the material?

> *Story from Rick*
>
> My dad was a schoolteacher. Although he was fun at home, I don't believe he was one of those "entertaining" teachers. He truly believed that the subject material in and of itself should be interesting enough to keep the students attentive. (By the way, he was a high school math teacher.) The problem with students these days, he would explain to me, is that all they want is to be entertained.
>
> Well, Dad, you're right, and you're wrong.

Once again: ***You do not have the right to be boring.***

The need to entertain

For good or bad, our MTV, 128-channel, HDTV-enhanced, special-effects society has become more entertainment-focused. People expect some level of zing in a presentation. But that is not necessarily a bad thing. Most of the time we talk, we present to a group of people who are, at least, somewhat interested in the topic. As a presenter, you need to take advantage of your audience's initial interest by giving them a reason to continue to be engaged in the topic. Therefore, there needs to be that added amount of interest level encouraged by well-placed, appropriate, planned "entertainment."

We think of it as using entertainment and humor to encourage and maintain an interest level that fosters learning. While most people want to learn, any encouragement we can give them is appreciated and helpful. The material may truly be boring — but it is also required or "recommended" by the boss. In all situations, but particularly in these cases, for the sake of kindness to humanity, make it fun.

The goal here is to use "entertainment" as a tool to improve the listeners' attentiveness, no matter what their level of interest in the topic. Your presentation could encourage active, positive listening, or it could be a deterrent to the audience members being mentally in tune with your topic. It's up to you. We suggest you use "entertainment" as an aid.

What is entertainment?

By entertainment, we don't mean telling jokes. Entertainment includes any technique that does not involve merely telling the audience the basics of the material. Interesting perspectives, fascinating quotes, bizarre analogies, and obscure stories will liven up any presentation. Use quotes that give a fresh look on the material, even if not originally intended for your topic. The key is to make any "entertainment" element relevant to the topic.

How much should I entertain?

There is a spectrum to consider when putting together your presentation. How much "entertainment" should be included? Aside from roasting a colleague at his or her retirement dinner, few of us will be asked to give a talk that is purely entertainment. Those people are called professional comedians or performers and they get paid accordingly.

A lot of the entertainment level will depend on the purpose of the speech. The more inspiring the talk, the more you can rely on various "entertainment" techniques. If your speech is heavy on the information and technical issues, you may not be able to "entertain" as much. However, remember our basic premise: *You do not have the right to be boring.* Your presentation style and the inclusion of interesting approaches in your talk, as described in some of the other chapters of this book, will have a great impact on the effectiveness of your presentation.

Thoughts on a couple types of entertainment

Although there are many ways to make your presentation more entertaining, here are a few comments on two of the more common methods used.

Quotes

Rick heard the following quote in a talk a number of years ago: "The definition of insanity is doing the same thing over and over again and expecting different results." It was interesting and made one think about the need for trying different approaches to a problem. It was an entertaining introduction to the topic. Since then, we have all heard this quote, or a variation of it, in about 13 million presentations. Okay, maybe, just maybe, that's an exaggeration. But this quote has been drastically overused.

Our approach to using quotes is never to use them from expected sources. Here are just a few ideas:

- Quote a high school friend or college buddy. But only tell the audience who it is after they have had a few seconds to think about whether they know the person quoted or should know him. Example: "As David Malecki once said, 'Life is not a musical.'" (On how things don't always work out the way you want.)

- Use quotes in nontraditional ways. Examples:

    o "There is nothing new under the sun." Solomon, c. 1000 BC. (During a presentation about basics that will not be new to them.)

    o "That which we call a rose by any other name would still smell as sweet." Shakespeare, *Romeo and Juliet* (Explaining that you may hear this concept referred to by a number of names, but it doesn't matter, they are all the same thing.)

- Quote yourself. Example: "It's a world of pies." Rick Drumm, 2004 (During an explanation of how funding for a particular program originates.)

As you can see, there can be many ways to use quotes that are intriguing or fun.

Stories

We covered stories in an earlier chapter, but here we are, more than ten chapters later, and it is still true. Stories bring a presentation to life. Here's our advice: Use them!

As described earlier, there are a few key concepts that should guide you when putting a story into your presentation. When you use stories, make them short and real, and have a point to them. Be creative with them and have fun.

Your Stories

In an effort to be entertaining, we would encourage you to "tell your story." We mean this in two ways. First, no matter what the topic, take your audience on an adventure. You do this by surrounding each topic with a story. Don't just tell them the facts; rather, tell them why such facts are important to them. Talk about the history behind the facts. Let them know the impact your topic can have on them. Their journey will be the result of your story.

Second, the best kinds of stories are the ones you have personally experienced. No need to use a story you heard on the radio this morning; instead, think about what has happened in your own life. We bet there are lots of untold but unbelievable stories just waiting for an audience.

These are just a few suggestions on integrating the element of entertainment in your presentation.

COACHING POINTS

✓ You need some entertainment in your presentation.
✓ Entertainment can take many forms.
✓ Use entertainment to improve the listeners' learning experience.
✓ Be creative in the form of entertainment you use in order to drive your point.
✓ Your entertainment elements should support and enhance your presentation.
✓ Have fun. If you are having fun, the audience probably is as well.

CHAPTER 20
PASSION

Loving what you do.

Like a salesperson who never uses the product that he or she is marketing, a presenter who doesn't believe in what he or she is presenting comes across bland at best, and a fake at worst. Would you buy a Ford from a dealer who drives a Toyota?

A Story from Rick

> I was preparing to take the licensing exam for my profession and got videotapes that reviewed the material. In the first tape, two gentlemen explained why the test was important and what it meant for the people taking it and for the profession. What they said was good stuff. But their presentation style was... let's just say I've talked to trees with more personality. These gentlemen were bland, monotone imitators of stone. Really exciting! For that setting, they didn't have to be fist-pumping entertaining, but at least they could have shown some passion as they explained why this exam and the professional licensing were important to us and society in general (which they are). Instead, their demeanor and lack of passion made me wonder if I was wasting my time and money taking this exam, and worse, whether I had chosen the right profession.

Show It!

Most of what we present has to do with our chosen vocations. If this field is not at least somewhat interesting to you, you need to change careers. So, assuming you do have some level of interest in the topic, our suggestion is – show it! You don't have to be a cheerleader or a sappy, gushing poet, but you do need to use your voice and body language to get your point across to the audience. If you don't sound excited about what you're presenting, others will find it hard to be interested in what you are saying.

No matter what your viewpoint on any issue or level of knowledge of any topic, one of the great aspects of public speaking in a professional setting is that you get the opportunity to share your point of view or what you know. Even though many people in today's world are hesitant about speaking in front of people, most everyone likes to tell other people new ideas or facts.

It is helpful to remind yourself why you are presenting this material. The answer may be, "My boss said I have to." Well, if that is the case, it would help a lot to remind yourself why you are speaking. You have something to say. You have information that will help people in their work or general life situation. You have ideas and concepts that may inspire people to improve. So, without being too deep and philosophical, we all need to remember that we do have something to contribute.

How do we show passion?

Passion is shown mainly through our tools as a public speaker. Speakers rely on voice and body language to relate that passion. We have a few earlier chapters that cover these topics. They are important and essential, so spend some time on these chapters. Whatever your skill level with your basic tools (your voice and body language), there is one important factor of which you are in almost total control – your passion.

A Story from Dan

Listening to someone talk with great passion coupled with knowledge about the topic can really have a tremendous impact. I remember watching the late North Carolina State college basketball coach, Jim Valvano, deliver a speech to a group of adults after his team had won its improbable national championship.

His passion for the game and for teaching young players about the life skills they learn by competing in sports really made me think about my role as a coach and the opportunity I have to influence young people. His sincere passion in his delivery was — and still is — very inspiring. His message was believable because he was so passionate about what he was saying.

Imagine that, after all these years, Jim Valvano's passion is still contagious.

"I've given it some thought..."

One key aspect of a presentation that will show the passion you have for the topic, and relate the importance of it to the audience, is to prepare well. This may seem simplistic, but think about it. A presenter who has slapped together a presentation the night before (or that morning) will likely be sloppy, disorganized, incomplete, and meandering. The more effort and time the speaker puts into preparing for the talk, the more the audience gets the sense that the speaker cares about what he or she is saying, and it tells them, "Pay attention! This is important to the speaker. This may be important to me, too."

How do you prepare? A great suggestion is to first read a good book on professional presentations, and, as fate would have it, that's what you have right in front of you now. We have written this book for you to improve your skills. And as you improve as a public speaker, people will take what you say more seriously. They will listen more attentively to what you have to say. They will want to hear more of your insight, wisdom, thoughts, or brilliance.

Therefore, work at improving your presentation skills – through reading and applying this book – and it won't just be your speaking skills that will improve. Your status will improve as well. And you will feel better about yourself, too.

COACHING POINTS

✓ Show your passion with voice and body.
✓ Talk about a subject you find interesting.
✓ Learn how to relate that passion.
✓ Prepare well for the topic and prepare well to speak.

CHAPTER 21
GETTING BETTER

Be the best you can be.

Self-Analysis

We know that many people think that the best time to consider improving your presentation is just before your next presentation. Oh, how wrong that is. And deep down, we all know that. It really only takes a few minutes to write down notes of analysis on all the different elements of your talk. What worked? What did not work? What needs more information? What can be deleted? Go through your presentation, element by element, and write down your impressions and analysis.

Whereas it is relatively easy to determine whether a joke or funny story worked – they laughed, it worked; they did not laugh, it did not work – it is more difficult to tell whether other elements of a presentation came across well. But it is not at all impossible.

You will have to be able to pick up on the clues the audience is giving in the terms of questions, physical cues, and attentiveness. First, realize that there will likely be one or two sleepers. You could be giving a presentation on "Surefire ways to get your spouse to do anything — yes, *anything* — you want" and still there will be a couple of people sleeping. That is the nature of people. There will always be people who are sleep-deprived, iron-depleted, overextended, and exhausted, or have narcolepsy. Don't worry about them, unless, of course, it is more than a very few who are snoozing. If that is the case, then you may want to reread this book, or take up magic tricks.

Facial expressions will tell you a lot about the different elements of your presentation. If you are explaining a technical procedure or process and your audience is looking at you like someone is describing the eleven dimensions of subatomic string theory in Greek, then that section will need additional work by using stories, analogies, graphics or props. (That is, of course, unless you are actually speaking in Greek about the eleven dimensions of subatomic string theory.) Make a note of that section of the talk right away. You can make presentation-improving self-assessments of your talk by observing audience responses.

Questions people ask or comments they make are another obvious source of enlightenment for you. Here are some thoughts:

Good Connection to Audience	Bad Connection to Audience
It looks like if I increase the heavy metals in my process, it will be more efficient.	I can't read that graph.
I haven't heard this concept before. Can you explain how I can implement it?	That slide makes absolutely no sense.
What is the time frame for this to help my situation?	Is it raining outside?
Could you come to my company and explain this to our employees?	When's lunch?

Sometimes it is not this obvious. But if audience members are asking for more information, further clarification, additional help, or, better yet, another presentation, they are focusing on the material and its use. This is always good.

If your "listeners" focus on how you are explaining it, how poor the visual aids are, or, worse yet, things completely unrelated to the topic, you have some work to do.

A Story from Dan

Several years ago, I was asked to speak to a group of high school students about having confidence and a strong work ethic. They knew nothing about me and I knew very little about them or their school. I was giving a talk I had done on several occasions and felt it was both good and appropriate for this group. I walked into a very defensive group of kids who looked like they were forced to be there and didn't really care what I had to say. I got the impression that some of them actually missed being in math class instead of having to listen to me. One student actually got up and walked out of the room. It threw me off of my delivery and I began to change the direction and content of my speech on the fly. This was not the best idea, and my adlib approach made the presentation a mess. The kids were unresponsive and the message was lost somewhere in the middle.

I learned a lot after I reflected and analyzed my presentation and realized I was not properly prepared for that type of response from that group. I was heavily critical of both my delivery and my content, quickly making notes on what I can do better in a situation like that. The best note I made to myself was never to repeat the same mistake again, and chalk that one up to a good learning experience. Constantly striving to improve, learning from past mistakes, and knowing that you always need to try to do better… that's the key to preparing and delivering a successful presentation.

Feedback from others

Another method in gaining insight into the effectiveness of your presentation and how to improve it is getting feedback from those who attend it. This is always difficult. If you simply ask someone, "How was my presentation?" they will respond, "It was good." This is the standard response that everyone, complete stranger to close friend, has been trained to say for the past 3,000 years. It was the response that Mark Antony got after his, "Friends, Romans, countrymen… " speech. It is what Lincoln heard after the Gettysburg Address. But before you think that your talk was in that category, remember that Bert from accounting was just given the same feedback after the presentation he just gave. The one that made seventeen audience members need to "go to the bathroom" and upon returning "accidentally" step in to the adjoining meeting room where someone was speaking on fourteenth-century revisionist history of the wooden plow. Compared to Bert, they realized, this was riveting.

An evaluation form is an option that many speakers will use. This works best for presentations such as training that last a few hours or more. Most people don't want to fill out an evaluation for a presentation that lasts barely longer than the time it takes to fill out the form. But even then, evaluation forms have their drawbacks. Many people fill them out by using a lot of four out of fives. In other words, they find another way to say, "It was good."

Another option for getting valuable feedback is to find a colleague who will give you good, honest comments on the quality of your presentation. This is not, we repeat, not easy to do. If you ask someone to give you **honest** feedback and then ask him how you did, he may answer, "It was good." Then you would say, "No, remember, I asked for honest, detailed feedback."

To this he responds, "Oh, right… uh… well… oh, I liked the story about the monkey."

"You did? What about it?" you ask.

And to that he replies, "It was good."

What you need is a co-worker or colleague who will be honest about your failures. At this point, we can hear the comments right through the pages of this book. "I got plenty of people that point out what I'm doing wrong." Okay, sure, we all do. But we need someone who will be give honest, specific, positive, and constructive feedback. Those people are not so easily found.

This person (or persons) should also be someone from whom you can take criticism. You really do need to find someone, or a few people, who will help you to get better and want you to get better. Your feedback person needs to have a good idea of what a good presentation looks like. (Maybe they've read this book!) You are looking for a trusted advisor.

A Story by Rick

Very shortly after being transferred to an office in a different state, my new boss, who arrived a week after I did, was making a presentation. I was one of only a few from our office in attendance. But my guess is that I was the only one taking notes, not on the subject matter, but on his presentation skills. I thought it would be helpful for him to get notes on what he did right – good opening, great analogy, etc. - to what he could improve – put down the glass, keep the momentum, use a story to make that final point, etc. On the way back to the office, I at least had the wisdom not to launch into a critique of his presentation. I did, however, mention that I took notes on his presentation techniques and I'd be glad to go over them with him. He never did take me up on the offer. I realized that since I had only met him less than a month earlier, he did not have the type of trust in me to accept constructive (and brilliant) feedback. I probably should have waited for a later time and a later presentation to offer my assistance.

Needless to say, it is difficult to find someone who can give good, honest feedback, but it is not impossible. And the benefits in terms of increased quality of your presentations will be great.

COACHING POINTS

- ✓ Make notes soon after your presentation on what went well and what didn't.
- ✓ Learn the clues audiences give by their questions and body language.
- ✓ Find a trusted colleague to evaluate you.
- ✓ Learn from your mistakes.
- ✓ Never repeat the same mistake.

CHAPTER 22
22 KEY STEPS

"And in conclusion..."

We have collected twenty-two key points from the pages of this book. Follow these, and your presentations will stand above those speaking before and after you.

We suggest working on a few at a time. So, the next time you have a presentation scheduled, select two or three of the following points, and make sure you work on them. Then, as you get those down, pick out a few more.

So, here they are, the top twenty-two:

1. There is no replacement for practice and preparation.
2. Be passionate about your topic.
3. Open with power and take command of your presentation.
4. Never exceed your allotted time, even if you have not covered all your material.
5. Talk to the people who are enjoying your presentation.
6. Establish eye contact with your audience (by using a concept outline).
7. Shake up the pace and be slightly unpredictable (use props).
8. Plan your transitions from topic to topic, subject to subject.
9. Use overheads and PowerPoint appropriately.
10. Take control over the technical operations of your presentation.
11. Know your audience.
12. Use humor to your advantage (self-deprecating humor works well).
13. Get the audience involved! Ask questions, ask for volunteers, make them stand, have them all make a paper airplane, etc.

14. Always have more material than you need. This allows you to venture off into unknown/unanticipated areas with knowledge and ends the day with people believing you have more information to give.
15. No need to narrate every action you make. Silence is not necessarily bad.
16. Be prepared for when things don't go right. Have a backup plan.
17. Become a master storyteller.
18. Involve your audience when- and wherever possible.
19. Evaluate yourself or have someone you trust offer constructive critiques of your presentations.
20. Work on your stage presence and your body language.
21. Have fun!

This last point could also be the first point:

22. You never have the right to be boring, so prepare to be engaging.

If you begin with the four E's of speaking and follow the basic points as outlined in this book, you are sure to improve on your next presentation. We look forward to listening to you when you are the next speaker.

Appendix A

Below is a sample concept outline that was used by Kam during one of his presentations. His keywords are highlighted in gray.

Hospital CEO/CFO meeting - HIPAA Compliance

1) Joke – father/son, donkey
2) Overview of regulations
   a) Why we need this law
      i) Twelve examples
   b) Define terms
      i) III
      ii) PHI
      iii) TPO
         (1) Explain each item
      iv) BA
   c) Patient has a right to inspect, copy and amend their medical records
      i) Example – OBGYN
      ii) Example – Patient complaint
      iii) Example – other phys records [example-repair shop]
   d) HIPAA privacy tree
3) Notice of Privacy Practices
   a) Requirements – Where to get copy (AHA Web site)
   b) Treatment for your own Web site
4) Minimum necessary
   a) Department story
   b) Forms
      i) Written
      ii) Oral
      iii) Electronic
   c) Nurse story
5) Business Associates
   a) Define – list out
   b) Example - Access

c) Deal with janitorial, volunteers who work offsite, messenger services, staff MDs
6) Security section
   a) Define terms – **risk analysis, standards, implementation specifications (42 – 22/20),**
   b) Differences between privacy and security
      i) EPHI – **story (parking lot)**
      ii) Read quote from regulations – p. 83383
   c) Required verses addressable
   d) Risk analysis
      i) **Threats, vulnerability, likelihood, criticality**
7) Review specifications
8) Q+A
9) Close – story re: OIG

Appendix B

A few examples of lessons that particular stories can show an audience.

Teamwork:

The Sting – A lot of people, some playing large parts, some small, work together to accomplish a goal.

Mystery Men – A small band of committed crime-fighters use their somewhat offbeat special skills to defeat the bad guys. A team does not have to be "superheroes."

An abundance of sports movies.

Creative Problem-solving:

Apollo 13 – History and the movie. Many different problems overcome on various systems of the failed flight.

History – Post it Notes. 3M Scientist Spencer Silver came up with what he thought was a useless adhesive. Four years later, a colleague who sang in a church choir needed markers in a hymn book that would hold their place without sticking securely. He used Silver's "useless" adhesive.

Mentoring:

Finding Forrester – An inner-city youth finds a mentor for his interest in writing in the most unlikely of people.

Responsibility:

History – Harry Truman, who, after his hat shop failed, worked twelve years to pay off the debt.

Integrity:

History – Dietrich Bonhoeffer, spoke out and worked against the Nazis in Germany. Friends got him out of Germany, but he insisted on returning to speak out further (and be involved in an assassination attempt of Hitler). He was eventually arrested and put to death days before the end of the war.

Being Lucky: (If it happens, take advantage of it.)

History – The inventions of the microwave oven, artificial heart, Scotchgard, Teflon, Krazy Glue, Popsicle, Velcro, safety glass, cellophane, penicillin.

Using Resources Wisely:

The Beverly Hillbillies – The TV show was about a family who had no grasp of what a wealth of resources (money, influence) they had at their disposal. How true that often is today. A speaker could even get everyone involved by having them sing the TV show's theme song. Start with the first line, and they'll join in!

Not listening to the critics (negative people) in your life:

History – Story of comments (as legend has it) from a screen test report on Fred Astaire. It read, "Can't sing. Can't act. Balding. Can dance a little."

Along with stories, or instead of stories of luck, could be considered for noticing the little things or making applications from the strangest places:

History – Swiss inventor George de Mestral noticed his dog covered with cockleburs. Observing them under a microscope, he saw natural hook-like shapes that grabbed onto the loops of the fur. It took eight year to perfect his new invention – Velcro. (There are many more interesting invention stories that are out there that teach persistence, observation, application, creativity, etc.)

Appendix C

Items to check before you talk

Temperature of the room – Warm? Cold?

Lighting
    Normal room lighting
    Presentation lighting
        If using a projector for a PowerPoint presentation or video, is the image washed out/visible to all?

Sight Lines – Can everyone see well? Are you going to block anyone's sight for a screen?

Microphone
    Working? Right volume level?
    Easily adjusted or put on (if mobile) without loud noise?
    Extra batteries available (if it uses them)?

Presentation – PowerPoint/Video
    Can you display it?
    Is image clear, large, visible, square?
    Can you change slides? – At computer? With remote? – Practice changing slides.
    Ease of bringing up, especially if there are other speakers?
    Laser pointer or other aids available and working?

Extras
    Are props placed and easily brought out and shown?
    Water available?

The Accountant

Kameron H. McQuay CPA/ABV, CVA is a principle and owner with the public accounting firm of Blue & Co., LLC in their healthcare practice. A frequent presenter at local and regional conferences, Kam's dynamic, humorous style encourages class participation and interaction. A powerful speaker whose personality holds his audience, Kam specializes in delivering technical, content rich programs, in a fun, inspirational and motivational style that will leave the group entertained, challenged and never the same. While Kam delivers more than 50 presentations per year, he maintains an ongoing client base of physicians, dentists and hospitals providing general financial, tax and consulting support.

Kam, Born in Chicago, Illinois, has a B.S. degree from the University of Evansville, and currently resides in Carmel, Indiana with his wife Debbie and their two children.

The Engineer

Rick Drumm is a Professional Engineer who has been a highway engineer for that past 14 years. He has a BS in Civil Engineering from Louisiana State University and an MS in Civil Engineering from Virginia Tech. Rick has lived all over the country, but for the past decade in Illinois and Indiana. He is frequently asked to speak at conferences and meetings by a wide variety of engineering associations and groups. Rick's particular interest is highway safety as he speaks entertainingly and passionately about reducing fatalities and injuries on our roads and highways. He is active in theater and in church, and he also loves a good game of basketball.

Rick has the joy of living with his best friend, his wife Susan, and their three children in Fishers, Indiana.

The Coach

Dan Kapsalis has had a successful athletic and coaching career in the sport of soccer that spans over 35 years from the youth level to Division I and the professional level. He currently holds the highest level of soccer coaching licenses from the top national organizations and is the former Director of Coaching for the State of Indiana. Over the past 20 years, Dan has trained over 20,000 athletes and educated hundreds of coaches and parents. Above and beyond coaching the game of soccer, Dan has published and produced original motivational prints and videos designed to improve team ethics, character and the importance of learning valuable life lessons through sports. He has delivered hundreds of presentations for various corporations, non-profit programs and national and local sports organizations and teams.

Dan, born in Chicago, Illinois with a B.S. degree from Indiana University, currently resides in the northern suburbs of Indianapolis with his wife Nancy and their six children.

Printed in the United States
84682LV00003B/209/A